OH FREEDOM AFTER WHILE

The Missouri Sharecropper Protest of 1939

A Curriculum Guide with Historical Background, Primary Sources, and Lesson Plans

Theodore D. R. Green and Lynn Rubright

We dedicate our work to our wonderful spouses,
who without their unending support,
this publication would have never come to fruition:
Mary Faith Green and Robert Rubright

TABLE OF CONTENTS

INTRODUCTION

This curriculum guide is designed to supplement the Emmy-award-winning documentary *Oh Freedom After While: The Missouri Sharecropper Protest of 1939* (co-produced by Webster University and University of Memphis) with classroom and individual activities to bring the film to life. In order to have a better historical understanding and to improve historical literacy skills, lessons have been designed with History's Habits of Mind from the National Council for History Education (NCHE) as well as meeting national and state standards in history and language arts. Each lesson contains a summary, outcomes, materials, strategies, and primary sources to use with students so that they get a well-rounded experience and become immersed in the materials.

Inside you will find primary source items including photographs, newspaper articles, oral histories, and other personal recollections of events that shaped the roadside protests in the Missouri Bootheel. Watching the three documentary segments before each of the three lessons will enhance student understanding and comprehension skills and make for a rich and vibrant learning experience. Explore photographs, get to know the people involved in this event, and learn about life in Cropperville through oral histories and stories from those who lived to tell about their experiences. We have included an additional historical literacy lesson using poetry, creative drama and reader's theater, and living history to enrich your language arts and performing arts curriculum. Here you will find activities that involve song, story, and performance.

It is our hope that use of this guide will provide students with a better understanding of civil rights issues in our country during the Great Depression and enable them to apply those lessons learned to our global society today. In essence, we hope to continue to support a more peace-filled and compassionate world through historical understanding and the performing arts.

With all good wishes,

Ted and Lynn

This curriculum guide has been underwritten with a grant from the Beatrice and David Kornblum Institute for Teaching Excellence, School of Education, Webster University, St. Louis, Missouri.

OH FREEDOM AFTER WHILE: THE MISSOURI SHARECROPPER PROTEST OF 1939

Historical Background

Text by Candace O'Connor, edited by Green and Rubright

One cold morning in January 1939, residents of **Southeastern Missouri** awoke to a startling sight. Overnight, more than a thousand **sharecroppers**—mostly African American, some white—had appeared alongside two state highways. With them were their families and their few meager belongings.

These sharecroppers had left the **Missouri Bootheel** cotton plantations where they lived and worked to stage this dramatic **demonstration**. They were protesting a new farm policy, the **Agricultural Adjustment Act**, which had come from the **New Deal** administration of **President Franklin Roosevelt**. A loophole in this policy allowed plantation owners to keep government money they owed the sharecroppers—if they fired their sharecroppers and hired new ones to take their place.

The organizer of the protest was **Reverend Owen Whitfield**, an African American minister, a former sharecropper himself, and vice president of the **Southern Tenant Farmers' Union**, which was dedicated to creating better conditions for

[3]

farm workers. Whitfield told the sharecroppers: "Take your eyes out of the sky, because someone is stealing your bread." He convinced them that a demonstration would draw public attention to their plight.

Not all the plantation owners treated sharecroppers unjustly. One planter, **Thad Snow**, had befriended Owen Whitfield, his wife, **Zella**, and their large family. He had even helped the Whitfields move into a new government housing project, **La Forge**, built in the **Bootheel** in 1937. La Forge was a dream come true for the Whitfields. Like other sharecroppers, they had lived in desperately poor conditions, despite backbreaking labor in the cotton fields.

Sharecroppers faced another threatening problem. Mechanical cotton pickers were being developed, making the sharecropping system obsolete. As the sharecroppers put it, "We are being tractored off the land." Some of them would join the **Great Migration**, a stream of people who fled the rural South for the promise of work in northern cities.

But in early January 1939, the protesters along the frigid highways were hungry and cold. The American Red Cross refused to help, calling the protest "a man-made disaster." Owen Whitfield could not join the demonstrators; he had to flee to St. Louis because of threats against his life. Still, day after day, the sharecroppers remained by the roadsides, huddling in tents. If they were fortunate, they used old iron cook stoves for warmth.

Gradually, the **demonstration** began to attract national attention—and to embarrass the state government. Reporters and photographers from major newspapers around the country traveled to the Bootheel to follow the crisis. Soon the governor sent state troopers to load the protesters into trucks and haul them away to different sites: a levee, a churchyard, and other places—all far out of public view. The demonstrators called them "concentration camps."

When **Lorenzo Greene**, a professor of history at Lincoln University in Jefferson City, Missouri, went to visit the demonstrators in the new camps, he described what he had seen to his classes. Students were so moved that they gave up their spring prom and donated the money to help. In St. Louis, activist **Fannie Cook** also organized a committee of citizens to send relief to the protesters. As months went by, some left the dismal campsites, but others stayed on; they had nowhere else to go.

The following summer, Cook's committee and the Lincoln University students donated money so that the remaining sharecroppers, still led by Owen Whitfield, could buy a parcel of land: ninety-three acres near Poplar Bluff, Missouri. Several hundred people—both black and white—moved to the site, which came to be known as **Cropperville**. The local sheriff warned them that he could not guarantee their safety in the face of hostility from the surrounding all-white community. In the end, no bloodshed occurred. Instead, the sharecroppers began tilling the land and building houses. At the beginning, there was much hunger and sickness—even some deaths—but Cropperville slowly began to take shape, with a school, a church, and community gardens.

Within a year, changes brought about by the protest were beginning to be visible. The governor held a conference at which Owen Whitfield, the planters, and officials talked about ways to help the sharecroppers. The federal government also got involved in the Bootheel, agreeing to provide new forms of assistance. Through the **Farm Security Administration (FSA)**, ten Delmo Homes communities for sharecroppers in the Bootheel were created for those needing a place to live.

But time went on, and the world began to change. Cropperville residents moved away to fight in **World War II** or to find better jobs. Finally, Owen Whitfield also moved to take a new church position. Ten years after it had begun, Cropperville was all but deserted.

Even though Cropperville did not endure, the roadside demonstration was a success. The story of the sharecroppers is an inspiring example of courage in the face of poverty and injustice. Not only did this protest lead to change on the state and national levels, but the sharecroppers also managed to build a better life for themselves and their children. In the words of the song that they sang during the protest, many sharecroppers did finally find "Freedom, oh freedom, oh freedom after while."

GLOSSARY

Activist—A person or group of people who campaign for some kind of social change. People who are involved in a protest, a political campaign, or social cause may be called activists.

Agricultural Adjustment Act (AAA)—New Deal law enacted in 1933 with the express purpose of bringing cotton prices back up to previous levels through farmer subsidies. A loophole allowed the farmers to avoid sharing the payouts with sharecroppers, thus factoring into the protest.

Anti-Strikebreaker Law—The Byrnes Act of 1936 was a law to prevent anti-strikebreakers from using threats or force on nonviolent picketers in labor disputes. It also prevented people from crossing state lines to disturb the picketers.

Barrel Staves—The sections of barrels used to create an entire barrel for goods to be stored and shipped.

"The Bootheel" in Southeast Missouri—The southeastern corner of Missouri, so called because it resembles the heel of a boot. The site of the 1939 protest.

Civil Disobedience—As a reaction to racial disparities, this was exemplified by street protests, commercial boycotts, unionization, and neighborhood uprisings.

Civil Rights Movement—The civil rights movement involved people from all backgrounds (religious, ethnic, socioeconomic) to protest injustices in work, home, community, and other areas. The sharecropper protest would be a motivation for the civil rights activism to follow in the 1950s and 1960s through today.

Committee for the Rehabilitation of the Sharecroppers—A group of activists based in St. Louis who, along with Fannie Cook and Owen Whitfield, helped establish Cropperville.

Concentration Camps—Embarrassed by the public nature of the protesters' demonstration, the Missouri state government moved participants out of view and into these areas: spillways, dance halls, and small African American churches.

Fannie Cook—Social activist from St. Louis who assisted the protesters with clothing, food, and support from others around the United States. Instrumental in getting materials for the school in Cropperville built by Quaker volunteers. Co-founder of the Committee for the Rehabilitation of the Sharecroppers.

Cropperville—An area created by Reverend Owen Whitfield and others after the sharecropper protest of 1939. The residents assisted one another in meager surroundings to tend the crops, school one another, and support the notion of family and equality.

Demonstration—A public gathering meant to communicate a desire to change a circumstance.

Desperation—Economic depression, greedy landowners, and legal loopholes contributed to the adverse living conditions and hopelessness of the sharecroppers.

Fair Labor Standards Act—The Fair Labor Standards Act of 1938 finally provided minimum wages and maximum hours for all workers.

Farm Security Administration (FSA)—A governmental agency created in the 1930s for the purpose of assisting displaced sharecroppers via resettlement.

"Furnish and Clutter"—The sharecroppers' belongings (pots and pans, clothing, furniture, and everything they owned).

The Great Depression—Worldwide economic crisis during late 1929 and throughout the 1930s leading to a substantial reduction of crop prices. This disproportionately affected sharecroppers and led to the enactment of the New Deal.

Great Migration—Between 1910 and 1970, six million black Americans moved from the rural South to other parts of the country.

Dr. Lorenzo Greene—Professor at Lincoln University, an all-black college in Jefferson City, Missouri, who encouraged students to assist the sharecroppers in southeastern Missouri.

John L. Handcox—Born in 1904, a tenant farmer who became a folk singer and poet, helped the sharecropper movement from Arkansas to Missouri and beyond. Handcox tried to better the lives of sharecroppers and energize the union movement.

Injustice—As manifested by the loophole in the Agricultural Adjustment Act of 1933, persistent racial discrimination and segregation, the injustice of the time inspired acts of protest culminating in the strike.

La Forge—Small Missouri Bootheel integrated farm community founded by the government in 1937, where the Whitfields and other sharecropping families moved.

Levee—One of the "concentration camp" sites chosen for protester relocation by the state government near Charleston, Missouri, on the banks of the Mississippi River.

Lincoln University—An all-black college in Jefferson City, Missouri, in the 1930s where students under the direction of Dr. Lorenzo Greene assisted the sharecroppers who were removed after the protest to the spillway and other sites out of public view.

Loophole—A means by white landowners of avoiding subsidy distribution to sharecroppers and appropriating land owned by the heirs of black farmers. A legal exception to the Agricultural Adjustment Act of 1933.

Mechanization of Agriculture—The process of machines replacing human labor in the farming fields. Led to the demise of sharecropping as a practice.

National Industrial Recovery Act—The National Industrial Recovery Act (NIRA) of 1933 provided codes of fair competition. It also attempted to bring in line wages and hours in businesses following these codes.

National Labor Relations Act—Also known as the Wagner Act, impacted firms and employees in activities affecting interstate commerce. However, agricultural laborers, government employees, and employees subject to the Railway Labor Act were excluded. This act provided workers the right to organize and join labor movements, and to strike.

New Deal Era—A series of economic programs enacted in the 1930s by President Franklin D. Roosevelt, intended to provide relief to the impoverished and reform to the domestic financial sector.

Poverty—Exacerbated by misguided government policy and greedy landowners, the living conditions of the sharecroppers were exemplified by a lack of resources.

Protest Music—Folk singers like John Handcox wrote about injustices stemming from economic adversity and racial hatred. The legacy was continued by the likes of Woody Guthrie, Pete Seeger, and many others.

Quakers—Members of a socially conscious religious movement that aided sharecroppers in Cropperville. They built the school building in Cropperville.

Red Cross—The American Red Cross, a disaster relief organization, called the sharecropper protest a "man-made disaster" and refused to help.

Roadside Demonstration—Peaceful demonstration of Missouri sharecroppers during January 1939 on Highways 60 and 61.

Eleanor Roosevelt—First Lady and wife of President Franklin Delano Roosevelt, who responded in writing to the sharecropper protest of 1939 through her weekly column, "My Day."

President Franklin Delano Roosevelt—President of the United States from 1933 to 1945, who met with Reverend Owen Whitfield and others to solve the unfair wages of sharecroppers and tenant farmers in the southern states.

St. Louis Urban League—Founded in 1918, the purpose of the Urban League was to eradicate racial tensions and improve the living conditions for African Americans in St. Louis.

Sharecropper—Someone who farms the land, tends the crops, and lives on-site but does not own the land. Also known as tenants.

Thad Snow—Plantation owner and writer who supported Owen Whitfield's pursuit of equal rights and decent working conditions for the sharecroppers in southern Missouri.

Southern Tenant Farmers' Union—Union formed to protect the rights of tenant farmers and sharecroppers in the South during the 1930s.

Spirituals—A religiously inspired musical tradition encapsulating African American protest, stemming from Civil War times. Often referred to as "Negro spirituals."

Lloyd Stark—Governor of Missouri during the late 1930s who instigated an investigation into the 1939 sharecropper protest. He ordered the protesters to be removed and dumped on a floodplain out of sight of motorists on Highway 61.

State Health Department—Missouri governmental agency responsible for removing the sharecroppers.

Tenant Farmer—Someone who farms and lives on the land but does not own the property.

Unions—Groups formed by workers with a common goal to protect their rights, improve their working conditions, and raise their status.

OH FREEDOM AFTER WHILE

The Wagner Act—The Wagner Act of 1935, also known as the National Labor Relations Act, was a very important labor law of the 1930s. This law included reenactment of the previously invalidated labor sections of the NIRA as well as a number of additions.

Walsh-Healy Act—The Walsh-Healy Act of 1936 made employees pay their workers the prevailing minimum wage and not less. The work week, as we know it today, standardized working hours to eight hours a day and forty hours a week, with time-and-a-half pay for additional hours. It also did not allow convicts or children under eighteen to work. It also made the workplace safer, with better safety and sanitation standards.

Reverend Owen Whitfield—Field worker, minister, and activist who led the sharecropper revolt of 1939 in southern Missouri and vice president of the Southern Tenant Farmers' Union. Co-founder of the Committee for the Rehabilitation of the Sharecroppers.

World War II—America's entry into World War II on December 7, 1941, forced citizens to ramp up war production. Many younger Cropperville residents enlisted in the military and/or moved away.

TIME LINE OF EVENTS

October 29, 1929	The stock market crashes, causing economic devastation to United States workers. This lasted for more than a decade.
1936	Great Migration begins with a stream of people fleeing from the rural South for the promise of better work in the northern cities.
1937	Agricultural Adjustment Act passes, paying parity to farmers. La Forge community started by federal government in the Bootheel. Owen Whitfield and his family move there with the help of Thad Snow.
1938	Plans get under way for the sharecropper protest in an aura of secrecy. Thad Snow is surprised to hear that Owen Whitfield intends to lead his people onto Highways 60 and 61 to protest farm conditions in the dead of winter.
January 8, 1939	*St. Louis Post-Dispatch* predicts walkout of sharecroppers.
January 10, 1939	Sharecroppers demonstrate on US Highways 60 and 61 over hundreds of miles in southeast Missouri and northern Arkansas.
January 24, 1939	Sharecroppers removed from roadside by Missouri state troopers by order of Governor Lloyd Stark to be placed in "concentration camps" away from public view on levee.
June 1939	Several hundred farmers, both black and white, move to Cropperville land purchased by Southern Tenant Farmers' Union.
December 7, 1941	US enters World War II as a result of Pearl Harbor attack.
1942	Delmo Homes started through the Farm Security Administration (FSA). Ten villages are built in the Bootheel for sharecroppers who needed a place to live—three black communities and seven white communities.
1942–1945	Cropperville residents move away to fight in World War II and to find new jobs. Owen Whitfield moves on to take a new church position.
1949	Ten years after Cropperville began, it was deserted.

Poster from Works Progress Administration, Division of Social Research, circa 1933

UNFAIR LABOR PRACTICES
Available in Black and White
(Part 1 of DVD, 0:00–22:32 min)

Introduction

Agricultural life in the South for both black and white poor sharecroppers was difficult. They faced tough conditions economically, geographically, and emotionally. Many experienced unfair labor practices despite federal and state laws to protect them. Some banded together to join unions to create a greater impact and improve their roles in a changing labor market.

Outcomes

As a result of this lesson, students will be able to:

1. Participate in a role play activity based on actual events in the documentary *Oh Freedom After While*.

2. Develop empathy toward the plight of the sharecropper.

3. Analyze early federal labor laws in the 1910s, 1920s, and 1930s.

Standards

This lesson plan meets the standards in literacy and social studies in the areas of Key Ideas and Details; Craft and Structure; Integration of Knowledge and Ideas; and Range of Reading and Level of Text Complexity.

Standards of Learning Based on History's Habits of Mind (NCHE)

1. Distinguish between the important and the inconsequential, to develop "discriminating memory" needed for discerning judgment in public and personal life.

2. Perceive past events and issues as people experienced them at the time, to develop historical empathy as opposed to present-mindedness.

3. Acquire at the same time a comprehension of diverse cultures and shared humanity.

Materials

- Five Biography Role Play Cards: Arthur Witman, Owen Whitfield, Thad Snow, Fannie Cook, and Zella Whitfield

- Federal labor laws from the 1910s, 1920s, and 1930s. See primary source documents on the Clayton Act, 1914; the Davis-Bacon Act, 1931; the National Industrial Recovery Act, 1933; the Wagner Act (also known as the National Labor

Relations Act [NLRA]), 1935; the Anti-Strikebreaker Law, 1936; the Walsh-Healy Act, 1936; and the Fair Labor Standards Act, 1938

- "Oh Freedom After While" reader's theater script
- Photos from the State Historical Society of Missouri

Strategy

1. Students will have viewed *Oh Freedom After While* (Part 1 of DVD, 00:00–22:32 min).

2. Students will analyze some of the federal work laws from the 1910s, 1920s, and 1930s.

3. Students will research and analyze historical newspaper accounts from archives of work practices in the South in regards to the tenant farmers and sharecroppers.

4. In small groups, students will research unfair labor practices taking place at the time, based on the federal labor laws of the 1920s and 1930s. They will compare and contrast the practices documented in newspaper accounts by reporters' and/or workers' experiences. See primary source documents on the Clayton Act, 1914; the Davis-Bacon Act, 1931; the National Industrial Recovery Act, 1933; the Wagner Act (also known as the National Labor Relations Act [NLRA]), 1935; the Anti-Strikebreaker Law, 1936; the Walsh-Healy Act, 1936; and the Fair Labor Standards Act, 1938.

5. Each group will then create a scenario of agricultural work scenes/tableaus based on primary source photos, documents, diary entries, and role play in groups for the class.

6. The larger class will then try to analyze and discover what type of unfair labor practices/discrimination occurred.

7. The whole class will have discussions on unfair agricultural labor practices of the time and their impact on both black and white workers in the South.

8. The class will then be called to action through participation in the reader's theater production of "Oh Freedom," the sermon leading up to the protest planned for January 12, 1939.

9. The teacher will ask for volunteers to take on various roles—Reverend Owen Whitfield and others—based on the notes from the reporter.

10. The rest of the class will have the reader's theater script in front of them to read along.

11. The student volunteers will practice a quick read through of their roles with the teacher.

12. The teacher will guide the entire class with the reader's theater script.

13. Students can then use the five Biography Role Play Cards to learn more about the important figures during the time.

14. Students will then discuss their thoughts and feelings about how Reverend Owen Whitfield inspired others to take up the cause in the dead of winter.

15. Students will then read through other documents of their choosing to decipher what may have inspired Reverend Whitfield and Thad Snow to join forces to support the sharecropper protest.

Primary Sources

Biography Role Play Cards

In groups or individually, students can use the five Biography Role Play Cards to learn more about the following people: Arthur Witman, Reverend Owen H. Whitfield, Thad Snow, Fannie Cook, and Zella Whitfield. They can read information silently and then discuss as a group and role play a scenario that relates to the sharecropper protest.

REVEREND OWEN H. WHITFIELD (1894–1965)

Reverend Owen H. Whitfield was a preacher, sharecropper, and union organizer for the Southern Tenant Farmers' Union, who rose to the position of vice president in the only union that welcomed black and white members. Later he traveled the country working for the Congress of Industrial Organizations (CIO), even meeting with President Franklin Delano Roosevelt in the White House, accompanied by his wife, Zella Whitfield. Born near Jonestown, Mississippi, Owen worked in the cotton fields as a child and helped his mother by picking up laundry and delivering ironing to her white customers. Owen was ambitious, valued education, and from a young age observed the racial injustice of the culture into which he had been born. Rather than become angry and bitter, he became a proponent of the social gospel, believing that blacks and whites could and must work together to gain economic equity.

Whitfield grabbed an education piecemeal, even attending some junior college classes in Mississippi before marrying Zella Glass when she was a teenager. As a socially conscious Baptist preacher, Owen used his remarkable gift for oratorical preaching to speak out on civil rights issues in the 1920s and 1930s. He planned the peaceful sharecropper protest in southeast Missouri in January 1939, and in June of that year he founded Cropperville, near Poplar Bluff, Missouri, as a way station for homeless sharecroppers, black and white.

THAD SNOW (1881–1955)

A brilliant, prosperous, renegade white farmer who owned a plantation near Charleston, Missouri, Thad Snow often wrote sarcastic commentary for the *St. Louis Post-Dispatch* on social injustice and farming conditions he encountered in southeast Missouri (which he called Swampeast, Missouri). He was instrumental in clearing 1,000 acres of cypress swamp and ultimately turning it into rich farmland. This region of rich land did not become cotton country until the boll weevil forced cotton planters from the South to move north to southern Missouri, bringing a southern agrarian culture of intense racial discrimination to the region. Snow became friends with African American preacher Owen Whitfield, even inviting the Southern Tenant Farmers' Union to organize his farm hands. He was a close observer of Whitfield's plan to organize the sharecropper protest of deplorable farming and living conditions, and he later often visited Cropperville, bringing game he had killed for the Cropperville residents. His biography, *From Missouri* (Houghton Mifflin, 1954), is a must-read for anyone interested in understanding the complex agrarian culture of the early twentieth century in southeast Missouri.

FANNIE COOK (1894–1949)

St. Louis writer, artist, and social activist, Fannie Cook was alarmed when she read the *St. Louis Post-Dispatch* article on Sunday, January 8, 1939, forecasting the sharecropper protest planned for the following week in southeast Missouri. She was thrust into action as subsequent news stories, with photographs by Arthur Witman, depicted destitute people of all ages lining Highways 60 and 61 to peacefully protest deplorable conditions sharecroppers faced as farm laborers.

As Cook was meeting with the director of the St. Louis Urban League to explore how she and other civic-minded St. Louisans might help, Reverend Owen Whitfield arrived at the Urban League. She immediately invited him to her home to explain the situation in the Bootheel that led to the demonstration. The Committee for the Rehabilitation of the Sharecroppers was started that day, with Owen and Fannie as charter members. Fannie Cook became good friends with Owen and his wife, Zella, and continued to work with them long after they established Cropperville. Fannie Cook was instrumental in having food and clothing contributed to the people as they worked during the summer of 1939 to begin gardens and build shacks from barrel staves contributed to the community. She also helped to find ways to furnish the new school, which was built by Quaker volunteers who came from around the country with books and desks. Her book *Boot-heel Doctor* (Dodd, Mead & Company, 1941) is a fictionalized account of the farm labor conditions that existed in southeast Missouri that led to the protest in 1939.

ARTHUR WITMAN (1902–1991)

Arthur Witman, an award-winning photographer on the staff of the *St. Louis Post-Dispatch* for thirty-seven years (1932–1969), used cutting-edge technology (35mm Leica camera) and helped develop photojournalism as a profession. More than 130,000 of Witman's prints, negatives, and transparencies are housed in the archive at the State Historical Society of Missouri. Through the sensitive and creative "eyes" of his camera, Witman established a body of work that reflects much of Missouri's visual history between 1932 and 1969. He documented the sharecropper protest of 1939 in the Missouri Bootheel, and later, using a Rolleiflex camera, took hundreds of pictures of the newly founded Cropperville (near Poplar Bluff, Missouri), which became home to about four hundred black and white refugees of the sharecropper protest, organized by Reverend Owen H. Whitfield. Arthur Witman's motto was: "Our eyes serve as the eyes of the reader."

ZELLA WHITFIELD (1900–1985)

During her life, Zella Whitfield bore fifteen children with Owen H. Whitfield. Six of the children are still living and contributing to society. Two of them, Elma Whitfield Statten and Shirley Whitfield Farmer, are preachers in addition to their other professions: Elma is a former nurse in Cape Girardeau, Missouri, and Shirley nurtures newborns in a St. Louis-area center focused on early language development. Zella was a tireless preacher's wife with a ministry of her own, as she served as the moral compass at Cropperville. It was Zella who understood Owen's passion for helping others before helping himself. She agreed to leave a comfortable home in La Forge, an integrated government farming community, where she enjoyed her first wooden floors, a porch, and electricity. She gave up this home to move her family to Kirkwood, Missouri, while Owen organized the sharecroppers. She insisted on moving to Cropperville when Owen was away organizing for the union around the country. She accompanied him to Washington, D.C., and met with Mrs. Roosevelt while her husband met with President Roosevelt.

Reverend Owen H. Whitfield
Photo by Arthur Witman. Used by permission and courtesy of the State Historical Society of Missouri.

LABOR RELATIONS ACTS
Congressional Digest, June–July 1993

Copyright and used with permission of EBSCO Publishing and the *Congressional Digest*

Federal Labor Laws

Present federal law regulating labor-management relations is largely a product of the New Deal era of the 1930s. While Congress has acted to raise the federal minimum wage and has considered labor law reform affecting both private and public employees, no major new labor laws have been passed over the past several decades.

Early Labor Laws

THE CLAYTON ACT

In response to pressure to clarify labor's position under antitrust laws, Congress, in 1914, enacted the Clayton Act, which included several major provisions protective of organized labor.

The act stated that "the labor of a human being is not a commodity or article of commerce," and provided further that nothing contained in the federal antitrust laws:

> shall be construed to forbid the existence and operation of labor . . . organizations . . . nor shall such organizations, or the members thereof, be held or construed to be illegal combinations or conspiracies in restraint of trade under the anti-trust laws.

RAILWAY LABOR ACT

In 1926, the Railway Labor Act (RLA) was passed, requiring employers to bargain collectively and prohibiting discrimination against unions. It applied originally to interstate railroads and their related undertakings. In 1936, it was amended to include airlines engaged in interstate commerce.

DAVIS-BACON ACT

In 1931, Congress passed the Davis-Bacon Act, requiring that contracts for construction entered into by the federal government specify the minimum wages to be paid to persons employed under those contracts.

New Deal Era Reforms

NATIONAL INDUSTRIAL RECOVERY ACT

In 1933, Congress passed the National Industrial Recovery Act (NIRA) at the request of newly inaugurated President Franklin Roosevelt. The act sought to provide codes of fair competition and to fix wages and hours in industries subscribing to such codes.

Title I of the act, providing that all codes of fair competition approved under the act should guarantee the right of employees to collective bargaining without interference or coercion of employees, was held unconstitutional by the US Supreme Court in 1935.

THE WAGNER ACT

By far the most important labor legislation of the 1930s was the National Labor Relations Act (NLRA) of 1935, more popularly known as the Wagner Act, after its sponsor, Senator Robert F. Wagner (Democrat from New York). This law included reenactment of the previously invalidated labor sections of the NIRA as well as a number of additions.

The NLRA was applicable to all firms and employees in activities affecting interstate commerce with the exception of agricultural laborers, government employees, and those persons subject to the Railway Labor Act. It guaranteed covered workers the right to organize and join labor movements, to choose representatives and bargain collectively, and to strike.

The National Labor Relations Board (NLRB), originally consisting of three members appointed by the president, was established by the act as an independent federal agency. The NLRB was given power to determine whether a union should be certified to represent particular groups of employees, using such methods as it deemed suitable to reach such a determination, including the holding of a representation election among workers concerned.

Employers were forbidden by the act from engaging in any of the five categories of unfair labor practices. Violation of this prohibition could result in the filing of a complaint with the NLRB by a union or employees. After investigation, the NLRB could order the cessation of such practices, reinstatement of a person fired for union activities, the provision of back pay, restoration of seniority, benefits, etc. An NLRB order issued in response to an unfair labor practice complaint was made enforceable by the federal courts.

Among those unfair labor practices forbidden by the act were:

1. Dominating or otherwise interfering with formation of a labor union, including the provision of any financial or other support.

2. Interfering with or restraining employees engaged in the exercise of their rights to organize and bargain collectively.

3. Imposing any special conditions of employment that tended either to encourage or discourage union membership. The law stated, however, that this provision should be construed to prohibit union contracts requiring union membership as a condition of employment in a company—a provision which, in effect, permitted the closed and union shops. (In the former, only pre-existing members of the union could be hired; in the latter, new employees were required to join the union.)

4. Discharging or discriminating against an employee because he had given testimony or filed charges under the act.

5. Refusing to bargain collectively with unions representing a company's employees.

The NLRA included no provisions defining or prohibiting as unfair any labor practices by unions. The act served to spur the growth of US unionism—from 3,584,000 union members in 1935 to 10,201,000 by 1941, on the eve of World War II.

ANTI-STRIKEBREAKER LAW

The Byrnes Act of 1936, named for Senator James Byrnes (Democrat from South Carolina) and amended in 1938, made it a felony to transport any person in interstate commerce who was employed for the purpose of using force of threats against nonviolent picketing in a labor dispute or against organizing or bargaining efforts.

WALSH-HEALY ACT

Passed in 1936, the Walsh-Healy Act stated that workers must be paid not less than the prevailing minimum wage normally paid in a locality; restricted regular working hours to eight hours a day and forty hours a week, with time-and-a-half pay for additional hours; prohibited the employment of convicts and children under eighteen; and established sanitation and safety standards.

FAIR LABOR STANDARDS ACT

Known as the wage-hour law, this 1938 act established minimum wages and maximum hours for all workers engaged in covered interstate commerce.

OH FREEDOM AFTER WHILE

Reader's Theater by Lynn Rubright

Inauguration of Franklin Delano Roosevelt, March 4, 1932.
FDRlibrary.marist.edu/archives/collections

Narrator: On January 7, 1939, Reverend Owen H. Whitfield calls Southern Tenant Farmers' Union members to a small church in Sikeston, Missouri. There, Whitfield encourages union members, black and white together, to walk out onto US Highways 60 and 61 to protest unfair treatment of sharecroppers and their deplorable living conditions.

Sing "Oh Freedom"* song: (together)

Oh freedom, oh freedom,
Oh freedom after while
And before I'll be a slave
I'll be buried in my grave
Take my place with those
Who loved and fought before.

Owen Whitfield: (dramatic preaching style)

The foxes have holes, and the birds of the heaven have nests, but the Son of Man hath no where to lay his head.

Owen Whitfield: And how many of you all got a notice to move?

All: Me preacher. I got it. I got it, brother preacher.

Owen Whitfield: And how many of you all got a place to live?

All: We ain't got no place. We ain't got no place to live!

Owen Whitfield: And that's why we're here. Let us all bear our burdens together. Let us make our plans.

All: Where we gonna go? 61 Highway! That's where we'll go! We can take our furnish and clutter out on the road.

Owen Whitfield: But suppose it be a raining!

All: (shouting) It ain't gonna rain!

Owen Whitfield: But suppose it be a snowing?

All: (more quietly) We'll be all right. It ain't gonna snow!

Owen Whitfield: But suppose it be a hailing and a lightning?

All: (shouting) We goin' anyway. Yea! We goin' anyway!

Owen Whitfield: Then we a goin'. We a goin' all together. We're gonna make an exodus, like the children of Israel. Remember, Moses got 'em to the Red Sea.

All: Yes, sir! We goin'. All together, we goin'!

Owen Whitfield: That's right. But there came old boss Pharaoh's riding horses in their chariots. And Moses raised his right hand and the waters parted and the children of Israel walked across the dry land!

All: That's right! We must make an exodus like the children of Israel, out onto Highway 61. Come rain, snow, hail, or lightning, we will go.

Sing "Oh Freedom"* song: (together)

Oh freedom, oh freedom,
Oh freedom after while
And before I'll be a slave
I'll be buried in my grave
Take my place with those
Who loved and fought before.

Narrator: Text is taken from Sam Armstrong's front-page article in the *St. Louis Post-Dispatch*, Sunday, January 8, 1939, based on his listening to Rev. Owen H. Whitfield addressing the Southern Tenant Farmers' Union members at the Sikeston, Missouri, church prior to the sharecropper protest and walkout onto Highways 60 and 61. The walkout took place on Tuesday, January 10, 1939.

A version of this traditional Negro spiritual was recorded by John L. Handcox, troubadour-organizer for the Southern Tenant Farmers' Union, on March 9, 1937, for the Library of Congress Archive of Folk Song by Charles Seeger and Sidney Robertson.

Tired family with children on roadside at night
Photo by Arthur Witman. Used by permission and courtesy of the State Historical Society of Missouri.

SHARECROPPER PROTEST
Freedom of Expression
in the Dead of Winter
(Part 2 of DVD, 22:32–36:42 min)

Introduction

Owen Whitfield and Thad Snow came from two different backgrounds, yet they supported one another in the sharecropper protest, even in the cold of winter.

How can people band together to create a better reality for the common good?

How does one inspire others to actually put their thoughts into motion?

Reverend Owen Whitfield had inspired both young and old to take a stand for a better tomorrow.

Outcomes

As a result of this lesson, students will be able to:

1. Understand the chain of events that led to the actual sharecropper protest of 1939.

2. Role play through reader's theater the reactions to the protest after January 12, 1939.

3. Experience what it means to "work for the greater good of others" through discussion of the tenets of community.

Standards

This lesson plan meets the standards in literacy and social studies in the areas of Key Ideas and Details; Craft and Structure; Integration of Knowledge and Ideas; and Range of Reading and Level of Text Complexity.

Standards of Learning Based on History's Habits of Mind (NCHE)

1. Recognize the importance of individuals who have made a difference in history and the significance of personal character for both good and ill.

2. Appreciate the force of the nonrational, the irrational, and the accidental in history and human affairs.

3. Understand the relationship between geography and history as a matrix of time and place, as a context for events.

Materials

• Eight photos of the roadside protest (see Roadside Protest Photo Key for details)

• Sam Armstrong's *St. Louis Post-Dispatch* newspaper account of Reverend Owen Whitfield's union meeting for black and white sharecroppers on Saturday, January 7, 1939.

- "Ten Million Sharecroppers," by Mildred G. Freed, *The Crisis*, December 1939.
- Article titled "What Makes the 'Good Community'?" (Penn State Extension)
- "In Plain Sight" and "Out of Sight" reader's theater scripts
- Thad Snow's biography (see Biography Role Play Cards, Lesson 1)
- Reverend Owen Whitfield's biography (see Biography Role Play Cards, Lesson 1)

Strategy

1. Students will have viewed *Oh Freedom After While* (Part 2 of DVD, 22:32–36:42 min).

2. Students will read Sam Armstrong's *St. Louis Post-Dispatch* newspaper account of Reverend Owen Whitfield's union meeting for black and white sharecroppers on Saturday, January 7, 1939. They will discuss what Reverend Whitfield had planned for the protesters to do.

3. The teacher will ask for volunteers to take the role of Reverend Owen Whitfield and others based on text from the reporter.

4. The class will be called to action through participating in the reader's theater production of "In Plain Sight," in which the protesters camped out in the dead of winter on Highways 60 and 61.

5. The rest of the class will have the reader's theater script from "In Plain Sight" in front of them to read along.

6. The student volunteers will practice with the teacher with a quick read through of their roles.

7. The teacher will guide the entire class with the reader's theater script.

8. Students will then discuss what options the protesters, the politicians, and aid workers had at the time.

9. Students will then analyze the eight large photos of the roadside protest using context clues. Students should use the primary source photo analysis worksheet from the National Archives to assist with this: archives.gov/files/education/lessons/worksheets/photo_analysis_worksheet.pdf.

10. The teacher should ask the students to identify specific jobs and activities at the roadside protest after analyzing the photos.

11. Students should also use their historical thinking skills:

- Chronological thinking
- Historical comprehension
- Historical analysis and decision-making
- Historical research skills
- Historical issues: analysis and decision-making

12. The class will be called to action through participating in the reader's theater production of "Out of Sight," regarding the removal of the protesters from Highways 60 and 61 to the spillway.

13. They will then discuss the reactions of various politicians and the local communities' actions after the removal of the protesters.

14. Ask the students to read, review, and reflect on "Ten Million Sharecroppers," by Mildred G. Freed, *The Crisis*, December 1939.

15. Students will then read over Reverend Owen Whitfield's and Thad Snow's biography to discern their views on community. (See Biography Role Play Cards from Lesson 1.)

16. Students will read the article titled "What Makes the 'Good Community'?" and try to decide what kind of community options were available for the protesters once they were removed from the roadside.

17. The teacher should hold a final class discussion to discuss the notion of "community" and how people banding together can make a difference.

Primary Sources

Roadside Protest Photo Key:

All photos by Arthur Witman and used by permission and courtesy of The State Historical Society of Missouri.

Roadside Protest photo 1: Women and children on side of highway in the evening
Roadside Protest photo 2: Children sleeping on the ground outside with dog
Roadside Protest photo 3: Men, women, and family with Reverend Owen Whitfield
Roadside Protest photo 4: Husband and wife trying to stay warm on roadside
Roadside Protest photo 5: Family and protesters gathered round the potbelly stove
Roadside Protest photo 6: Protesters gathered around an evening fire
Roadside Protest photo 7: Protesters with their "furnish and clutter" on Highway 60/61
Roadside Protest photo 8: Small child eating meal outside in winter

Women and children on side of highway in the evening

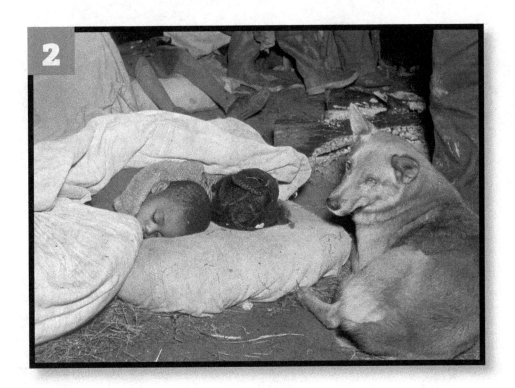

Children sleeping on the ground outside with dog

Photos by Arthur Witman. Used by permission and courtesy of the State Historical Society of Missouri.

Men, women, and family gather to support one another during the protest

Husband and wife trying to stay warm on roadside

Photos by Arthur Witman. Used by permission and courtesy of the State Historical Society of Missouri.

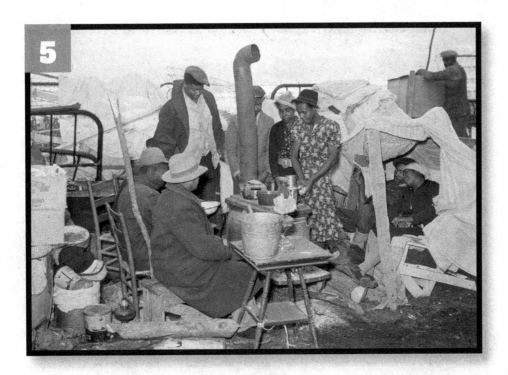

Family and protesters gathered round the potbelly stove

Protesters gathered around an evening fire

Photos by Arthur Witman. Used by permission and courtesy of the State Historical Society of Missouri.

Protesters with their "furnish and clutter" on Highway 60/61

Small child eating meal outside in winter

Photos by Arthur Witman. Used by permission and courtesy of the State Historical Society of Missouri.

Sam B. Armstrong's *St. Louis Post-Dispatch* article, Sunday, January 8, 1939. Published with permission of the *St. Louis Post-Dispatch*.

SHARECROPPERS, ORDERED EVICTED, TO CAMP ON ROAD

Mass Exodus From Homes of 1700 Southeast Missouri Workers Arranged for Tuesday.

'MAKE NO TROUBLE,' LEADER TELLS THEM

Community Chiefs to Direct March to U. S. 61 and Relief Committees Named at Mass Meeting.

By SAM B. ARMSTRONG
Of the Post-Dispatch Staff.

SIKESTON, Mo., Jan. 7.—Rain or shine, foul weather or fair, hundreds of sharecroppers of the Southeast Missouri cotton country who received eviction notices at the year end plan to move with their families to the barren brown right-of-way of U. S. Highway 61 in an organized exodus Tuesday, the last day of grace under the law.

With prayers and hymns, 350 representatives of more than 1700 in seven counties who were said to have been given notices to move met yesterday at the First (Negro) Baptist Church on the "other side of the railroad tracks" in Sikeston, discussed their plight and determined their course of action.

"The foxes have holes and the birds of the heaven have nests; but the Son of Man hath not where to lay his head," quoted Owen H. Whitfield, Negro tenant on the La Forge resettlement project, who finds time between cotton chopping and picking to fill several pulpits in the district.

None Has Place to Go.

The proceedings partook of the character of a church service as well as a mass meeting called to meet a crisis. Whitfield's discussion of their position and his frequent analogies drawn from the Scriptures evoked choruses of "amen," from his audience, mostly Negroes, but with a scattering of white sharecroppers. Often, however, solemnity gave way to gales of laughter as he made some sally in the vernacular of the cotton fields.

"How many of you got a notice to move?" asked Whitfield. Virtually all raised their calloused hands and began a chant of "Me, me."

"How many have got a place to go?" The hands dropped and silence fell.

"That's why we're here," Whitfield went on with solemnity. "Let us all bear our burdens together. Let us make our plans. Take a turkey or a goose—anything that flies has to squat first.

"Where we goin' to go?"

"Sixty-one Highway," came the answer from a half-dozen delegations.

"Suppose it be rainin'?" Whitfield prodded. "No, no, it ain't a-goin' to rain." The answering measured chant of the rich, melodious voices rose as he cathechized.

"Suppose it be snowin'?" "No, no, it ain't a-goin' to snow."

"Suppose it be hailin' and lightnin'?" "It ain't a-goin' to hail and lightnin'. But we're going anyway."

Whitfield's white teeth gleamed in a smile of satisfaction at the response. He, too, although he was secure in his own house, would join them and would return to his family only when their needs were provided.

"We Also Make an Exodus."

Attentively, his listeners followed him as he related the story of the exodus of the Children of Israel from Egypt to the land of Canaan.

"And Moses got 'em to the Red Sea," he said, "and they made camp there. But here came old Boss Pharaoh's ridin' bosses in their chariots. And Moses raised his hand, and the waters parted and the children of Israel walk across on dry land. And Moses raised his hand again as the riding bosses follow, and the seas close over them.

"We also must make an exodus. It's history repeatin' itself in 1939."

"That's preachin'! Amen!"

But Whitfield, and another part-time Negro preacher, R. H. Bradford of the Drinkwater community in Mississippi County, cautioned that they must be orderly.

"We must obey the law, get out when the notices say, and make no trouble," Whitfield emphasized. "And we don't want to break up any deal any cropper has made with his boss. If he's got a share-croppin' deal for next year, let him sit right tight. And if I hear any of these sharecroppers sayin' we're causin' trouble between croppers and their bosses, he's goin' to get a mouthful of my fist."

How Planters Save.

Since the Agricultural Adjustment Administration's cotton curtailment program has been in effect, an increasing number of planters have sought means to obtain a larger share of the Government payments, Whitfield explained. They have found, he said, that by changing the status of share croppers to that of day laborers at 75 cents to $1 a day for about 120 days a year, they can produce cotton more cheaply and remove the necessity of sharing the crop reduction payments with the sharecroppers.

In some instances, he added, the sharecropper's part of the Government payment would amount to more than $100. A planter with about 200 acres of cotton said he might save $1500 to $2000 a year by such a change. Eviction notices issued this winter in unprecedented numbers, provided a record showing there are no croppers to share Government payments. Some sharecroppers have received tacit approval of their remaining in their shacks in spite of eviction notices, it was said, but indignation at the further reducton in low sharecropper incomes was a large factor in bringing about yesterday's meeting.

Community Leaders Named.

"You've got no place to go and the only thing left for us is to move quietly like good citizens to the highway," Whitfield summed up. "People maybe will see what we're up against. Maybe we'll get our names in the paper for something besides stealing hogs and corn.

"And don't let anyone say we're tryin' to make trouble. It seems to be almost a criminal offense to wake people up so they take peaceful group action. That's why I left my store-bought clothes home and wore these—I may have to crawl in a log most anytime."

Leaders were designated in the various communities to organize marches to the highway, and committees were named to plan action for relief.

Then again the chorus rose in a final hymn before adjournment:

"I know the Lawd has heard my cry, and pitied every groan.
Long as I live, when trouble 'rives, I'll hasten to His throne."

December. 1939   367

Ten Million Sharecroppers

By Mildred G. Freed

NEW YEAR'S day to some ten million sharecroppers is the day the "bossman" hands them their eviction notices.

Last January 10, last day of grace after eviction notices had been served, 100 miles of highway along Route 61 in "Swamp-East" Missouri were covered with sharecroppers, white and Negro.

With sticks of furniture piled beside the fence, with women and children sleeping through sleet and through snow, almost 2,000 homeless sharecroppers huddled beside the ice-bound highway.

Two thousand evicted sharecroppers with nowhere to go.

Highway 61 is one of the most travelled highways in the country. People going east and west, people going north and south saw these shelterless families and stopped to talk to them. Newspapermen came down and asked questions. Photographers flashed bulbs in their faces as they slept.

But local planters weren't pleased with this highlighting of their sins. They angrily called for an "impartial investigation". They got it. The F.B.I. proved that the leader of the demonstration was a man who had been a sharecropper for 35 years—Rev. Owen H. Whitfield. (The planters, still dissatisfied. I was told, then began to yell for a Dies' investigation.)

These sharecroppers suffered the sleet and the snow because they were determined to show the country just what sort of conditions surrounded them. They were convinced that once the American people were aware of their plight something would be done about it.

Something was.

One night the State Health Doctor came out to these people living beside the frozen roadside, poked around their teeth and declared. "These people are a serious menace to public health—they must be removed."

Highway patrolmen and vigilante committees snapped into action. Thirty-two families were dumped into an old two-room abandoned building; twenty-three families, white and Negro, were piled on top of the Mississippi levee: twenty-five families were crowded into an unused church. A few weeks later the owners of these buildings instituted proceedings against these "tresspassers"!

Eviction day draws near for the sharecroppers on the plantations of the South. This account of the plight of 96 families is a fair picture of the predicament of the others

96 Families Still Live There

Today on the banks of the Little Black River, on their 93-acre tract of barren land in Butler county, live 96 white and Negro families—the nucleus of the roadside demonstration. (This land was bought for them by a group of sympathizers in St. Louis in conjunction with UCAPAWA, the C.I.O. Union to which these sharecroppers belong.) They live in barrel-stave huts and rag tents. The occasional army tent—there are several ex-servicemen in the group—looks very spic and span in contrast to the dreary mud-chinked "homes" of the others. Although there are over 50 log-cabins built on the partially-cleared timberland, only the odd one has a roof. I inquired about this and a tall gaunt man replied, "We's hopin' gonna be some way t'git nails an' roofin befo' the cold comes. Cain't seem t'git nails without money nohow."

Food at the camp is obtained from relief. "Relief" consists of four pounds of corn grit (chicken feed looks more appetizing): four pounds of meal and two pounds of beans. This has to last a family, often as large as ten, for a whole month.

Meals are eaten twice a day on a homemade table by the side of the tent. I sat on a chair that was a wooden frame with a few stray wires that kept me from falling through. Drum barrels added to the number of chairs. The children ate standing up—digging their bare toes into the dust.

In the center of the table was a plateful of soupy corn grit; a sorry-looking mess of crumpled beans; a pasty concoction of meal and water is baked in the wood-burning stove and called "bread". One bite and the sickly smell of the dough cooked without salt or grease upset my stomach so that I had to smoke innumerable cigarettes to keep from insulting my hosts in a manner beyond my control.

Naturally this shockingly ill-balanced diet leads to bad health. Most of the children at the camp have rashes.

Mothers, with the inevitable exhaustion of sharecroppers' wives, feed their children at the breast for two and three years—they have nothing else to feed them. Noon is lunchtime in New York, but just another hour in the sharecropper camp.

There was a young married woman at the camp who had been feverishly ill ever since she had come to the camp three months ago. She was suffering from her third miscarriage within the year.

"Why don't you get a doctor to see her?" I asked with the naive confidence of the North.

"Private doctor he won' come 'cause we ain't got no money and county doctor he said he ain't never gonna help us." (Later I learned from a local newspaperman in Poplar Bluff that the county doctor is a brother of a large landowner in Mississippi county, where the roadsiders staged their demonstration. He said he'd "be damned" if he'd ever help the camp in any way. Camp delegations to see him proved fruitless.) The patient was deliriously ill. Her husband went to Poplar Bluff (15 miles) for a doctor who agreed to come for $5.

The worried crowd gathered outside the rag tent made way for the doctor. Inside, the tent was completely filled with two large beds and a battered trunk. A few women sat on one bed. The patient tossed feverishly in the other. At the foot of her bed her husband sat. silent.

The doctor was brief. "What you need. young lady." said he in a professional manner, "is a light diet of milk. eggs, orange juice,—umm, perhaps a little corn flakes."

"But she ain't got nuthin but corn grit. doctor," said the husband.

The doctor left a few fever pills, took his $5 and hurried off.

For the next ten days or so the patient received a few basic food stuffs. Her fever dropped and by the time I left the camp I thought she was completely cured. But her tiny store of food was soon exhausted. A week later she died.

The Red Cross

"Have you asked the Red Cross to help?" I asked.

"Red Cross they said they cain't help 'cause this is a man-made disaster."

(Continued on next page)

The Crisis

"Isn't war a man-made disaster?" I couldn't help interjecting.

"When I said that they kicked me out."

And the phrase "man-made disaster" applies here—as it does to war. These sharecroppers are a part of what President Roosevelt called "our economic problem No. 1." Congress passed a parity bill to help them. Under the Cotton Crop Control, planters can only grow a certain amount of cotton. The government pays them per acre for the land that lays idle. The law also says the sharecropper—who works for a percentage of the amount of cotton he picks, sometimes as little as three-eighths—should get the same per cent of the government parity payment.

But too often he doesn't. Many planters, hard-up themselves, figured out the following "economical" plan.

They evicted their sharecroppers, whom they had to feed all year on credit (sharecroppers work to pay the landlord back for the food eaten between cotton seasons. Of a group of 2,000 families surveyed in Alabama, 61.7% broke even; 26% "went in the hole"; and 9.4% made a profit of from $70 to $90 a year.)[1]

The planters then keep the government payments and during the cotton season, they re-hire their former sharecroppers as day laborers. Planters find this system much cheaper because they only pay the day laborer from 40¢ to $1 a day—with wife and children picking too. Out of this amount the day laborer has to pay rent and buy food, usually at the planter's store. In between seasons these homeless families have no money and nowhere to go.

The fight against becoming day laborers led these evicted sharecroppers to "sit down" in the State highways last January. These same conditions, and the increase in the use of tractors, according to government estimates, will make an additional 40,000 sharecroppers homeless each year.

"Forty acres and a mule" is the American conception of what is needed to adequately support a family. On these 93 acres of the camp live 96 families with nowhere to go.

Leader Whitfield

Rev. Owen H. Whitfield, the leader of last year's roadside demonstration is a thin, light-skinned man with Indian features. When anyone asks his nationality he laughs:

"Y'see its this-a-way," he'll begin. "On m'mother's side, m'gran-mother,

[1] From a study in 1932 published in "Shadow of the Plantation" by Dr. Charles S. Johnson.

she were Creole Indian; m'gran'father, he were white man. But on m'father's side, m'gran'mother, she were Indian 'nuther tribe, an m'gran'father, he were African. And so," (this always tickles him) "I ain't sure what nationality I is exactly but I know its American."

The mother of ten children, Mrs. Whitfield is a charming, youthful-looking woman sincerely interested in helping her people.

Born in a drab sharecropper's cabin, their earliest recollections are of the cotton patch where they struggled along behind their parents picking cotton.

The Whitfield family found their first security on the LaForge Project. But, says Rev. Whitfield, "If'n I were in the Garden of Eden an I heard a lil baby cryin on the other side o that door, I couldn't be happy less'n I got that baby in too."

And so when almost 2,000 sharecroppers were evicted last Janunary, he left his home to lead his people " an show the country what condition they's in."

Today he is a District President of UCAPAWA. "I believes in this here union," he will tell you, "as bein th'only way t'raise the people up out'n their slavery." And that sentiment is echoed by the whole camp.

"But what would you like to see done for the 500 people at the camp?" I asked.

"I'd like t'see them put back on the land on a gov'ment project," Whitfield answered, "like the LaForge Project."

The LaForge Project is a self-liquidating one under the Farm Security Administration. It consists of 100 sharecropper families, white and Negro, who would otherwise have had to go on relief. The government furnished their homes and tools on long term payments, and they farm the land cooperatively, although each family has its own little home it will eventually own.

Everything is under government supervision. The men are taught to care for the soil. The women are

———

Hate

By PAULI MURRAY

Heaven hates with cosmic ire—
The star points break,
The earth's core cracks
And fire-tongued mountains
Leap upon a sleeping valley.
But when man hates
His clumsy hands spill only human blood,
And where, in some quiet land
White goats have danced upon a hill
Or children gathered flowers,
A thousand puny skulls by heaven unseen
Give feast to flies and maggots.

taught to preserve fruits, fish, etc. Children are sent to schools to make up for their too-often neglected backgrounds.

The F.S.A. has more than a dozen such rehabilitation projects already started in the South. Some are farmed cooperatively; others are based on individual ownership. Some start with sharecroppers who advance to the renter's class and, if they make good, eventually own their land.

Travelling through the drab sharecropper areas in the South, the white paint, the new methods of subsistence farming which replace the soil-depleting one-crop system of the cotton states, all prove that the self-liquidating projects of the F.S.A. offer America the hope of adjusting this tremendous economic problem of the South.

As one of the sharecroppers at the camp puts it, "Seems like there's enough land in this here country fer everybody t'live comfortable. All we want is t'be able t'use the gov'ment's idle land t'raise food so's we could keep the children from starvin."

A new year is coming.

What hope can the new year bring to the thousands of sharecroppers who again face eviction this January? I received a letter from Rev. Owen H. Whitfield written from the field Nov. 14, 1939:

"Our people on farms are getting eviction notices by the hundreds. Those who are not evicted outright must accept day labor at starvation wages or get out without written notices. And you can see what this means. It means we will be faced with another exodus with no place to go. . . ."

NEXT MONTH

"Britain's Black Background"

By J. A. ROGERS

•

The first of three articles

From Penn State Extension web article "What Makes the 'Good Community'?" (August 8, 2017). Reprinted with permission.

WHAT MAKES THE "GOOD COMMUNITY"?

Did you ever stop to think about what makes your community a good place to live?

What is it about your community that makes current and future residents and businesses want to locate, live, work, and/or play there? Evidence suggests that businesses and residents place considerable importance on community characteristics that go far beyond simply a vibrant economy. Importantly for many communities, a strong social and aesthetic foundation is critically important to building a healthy and sustainable economy—and not necessarily the other way around.

While everyone is likely to answer the questions above a bit differently, research over the years suggests a number of commonalities in our preferences that are worth considering in our efforts to build strong and vibrant communities. Looking at your community through the lens of these considerations may well suggest strategies for strengthening your community's social, economic, and environmental well-being—and long-term success.

While there's a good bit of social science research that addresses one or more aspects of what we're looking for in the "good community", two studies are particularly relevant.

Perhaps best known, David McMillan and David Chavis (1986), in their analysis of previous studies found that four factors consistently show up as community attributes we all look for in a good community.

- **Membership**—that feeling that part of us is invested in the community, that we have a right to belong and feel welcome

- **Influence**—that sense that we have some say in the community issues that affect us and that our perspectives are appreciated and respected

- **Integration and fulfillment of needs**—based on the notion that the community has numerous opportunities for both individual and social fulfillment including basic needs, recreation, and social interaction. Some scholars have referred to this as meeting the needs of [sic] whole person in all our roles (e.g. goods, services, recreation, desirable social interaction activities, etc.).

- **Shared emotional connection**—based in part on shared history or sense of community and quality of interactions within the community

The second study comes from the Soul of the Community Project conducted in twenty-six communities across the nation by the Knight Foundation and Gallup (2010). The focus of this work was to look at those factors that facilitate "community attachment." *In addition to highlighting individual factors, they found that those communities with the highest levels of community attachment also had the highest rates of growth in local gross domestic product.*

The ten community characteristics that most influenced community attachment (in order of importance) were: **social offerings, openness, aesthetics, education,** and **basic services.** While there were some differences in the relative strength of each of these factors across the twenty-six communities, these five factors consistently had the strongest influence on feelings of attachment. Other important but somewhat less influential factors included **leadership, economy, safety, social capital,** and **civic involvement.**

Taken together, this and other research provides strong evidence for communities to pay close—and specific—attention to the social as well as economic conditions in their communities. While these are often related, the evidence suggests that businesses and residents are clearly looking for community characteristics that go far beyond simply a vibrant economy. Perhaps even more importantly, it seems clear that a strong social and aesthetic foundation is critical to building a healthy and sustainable economy—and not necessarily the other way around. How would you assess your community on each of these characteristics? And what strategies can you put in place to begin strengthening this foundation?

IN PLAIN SIGHT
Sharecropper Protest on Highways 60 and 61
Reader's Theater by Lynn Rubright

Directions:

1. Select students to participate in this reader's theater on points of view to the sharecropper protest in southeast Missouri in January 1939.

2. Do a quick run-through before doing the actual performance in class.

3. Project pictures of the protest on the wall as the script is read by students.

Voices:

John Handcox, Southern Tenant Farmers' Union troubadour-organizer; reporter, *Enterprise-Courier*, Charleston, Missouri; reporter, *Kansas City Star*; reporter, *Chicago Daily Record*; Red Cross worker; Missouri Governor Lloyd Stark; group of sharecroppers

John Handcox (Southern Tenant Farmers' Union): (sings or chants)
> Raggedy, raggedy are we,
> Just as raggedy as raggedy can be.
> We don't get nothing for our labor,
> So raggedy, raggedy are we.

Reporter (*Enterprise-Courier*, Charleston, Missouri):
Very few of the campers know why they are camping along the highways. In a general way they are objecting to "conditions." Most of those interviewed have an abiding faith that someone—the government or some agency—is going to furnish them with tents, houses, food, fuel, and a better economic condition.

John Handcox: (sings or chants)
> So hungry, hungry are we,
> Just as hungry, as hungry can be.
> We don't get nothing for our labor,
> So hungry, hungry are we.

Reporter (*Kansas City Times*):
Radical agitators have gone among the sharecroppers of Missouri spreading discontent and unrest—just like they did in eastern Arkansas, Tennessee, and Mississippi. These organizers urged tenants and sharecroppers to organize and press their demands for higher wages and better working conditions.

John Handcox: (sings or chants)
So landless, landless are we,
Just as landless as landless can be.
We don't get anything for our labor,
So landless, landless are we.

Reporter (*Kansas City Times*):
These problems of destitute sharecroppers lining the highways in southeast Missouri have been brought to national attention by photographs and stories of their lives. But the solution to the problems down here must be reached by a long process of betterment in which education, industry, self-reliance, and proper ways of living will have to play the dominant part.

Reporter (*Chicago Daily Record*): (outraged, demanding help and justice)
Something must be done to help these poor people—men, women and children! Send protests to Governor Lloyd C. Stark in Jefferson City, Missouri, urging that evictions stop and immediate aid be sent to these sharecroppers. Write to the Red Cross! Demand that it act! And let the trade unions send observers down there to see that terror is not the landlords' answer to their protesting sharecroppers.

Red Cross Worker:
We have studied the situation in southeast Missouri, and we have determined that it is a man-made disaster. Therefore, we will not send tents and provide food and clothing.

Lloyd Stark (Governor of Missouri):
Get those people off the highways! They have no shelter, food, or sanitation! Call it a health hazard. Insist the planters take their sharecroppers back onto their land. Use state troopers and trucks to haul the rest away. All this protest business is giving Missouri a bad name. It has got to stop!

John Handcox:

So the sharecropper protest was officially called a health hazard. Urged by the governor, landowners took most of the protesters back to live in the squalid shacks on the land they had left. But state troopers packed the remaining four hundred men, women, and children—black and white—into trucks and took them to concentration camps on the levee and in churchyards out of public view. What would become of these homeless, destitute people?

All:

So pitiful, pitiful are we,
Just as pitiful as pitiful can be.
We don't get nothing for our labor,
So pitiful, pitiful are we.

OUT OF SIGHT
Sharecropper Refugee Camps in 1939, Southeast Missouri

Reader's Theater by Lynn Rubright

Directions:

1. Select students to participate in this reader's theater on life in the sharecropper refugee camps in southeast Missouri in 1939.

2. Assign seven voices to students: four storytellers, a planter, a woman, and a union organizer.

3. Do a quick run-through before doing the actual class performance.

4. Project pictures of the sharecropper refugee camp on the wall as the script is read by students.

Storyteller One:

Missouri Highways 60 and 61 are free of protesting sharecroppers. Governor Stark demanded these people be moved to where they cannot be seen, where they cannot be an embarrassment to the state of Missouri.

Planter:
Where are they? Where were they taken?

Storyteller Two:
I know where they are. The displaced sharecroppers are living like refugees
in a hostile country—scattered in hungry camps in small Missouri towns near
Charleston, New Madrid, and Wyatt. In Dorena, they are hidden in a swamp along
the river.

Storyteller Three:
The Sweet Home Baptist Church is filled with makeshift bedding piled on boards
and springs between the pews. In the churchyard, families cook on stoves in the
raw spring air and the cold mud. Flapping sheets of sackcloth tied to poles try to
protect them from the wind. Grown-ups eat a little salt pork, beans, and bread.
Oatmeal is saved for the children but hardly ever served with milk.

Woman:
Some man brought us milk once, but then he heard about some of us getting
a government check. And it seems like ever since, folks thinks we are taken
care of all right. A planter and his wife came and tried to get us to sign over our
government checks that are kept at the agency. But the union man said, "Don't
sign a thing." We didn't.

Union Organizer:
The guards let me deliver a carload of food contributed by union members
who are little better off than these homeless sharecroppers. But they only let us
because a government observer from Washington, D.C., came to see how folks are
living down here.

Planter:
These spies from Washington come snooping round down here. What business is
our trouble down here to them? We shoulda stoned them to death.

Union Organizer:
I got me a job in town for fifty cents a day. But my real job is signing up folks to
join the union. But at that job, I can only work at night under cover of darkness.
Four hundred folks already joined. Another fifty-two joined before I left. Just like

Owen Whitfield told us to do. I have a letter here from Reverend Whitfield. Come listen.

Union Organizer: (reading Owen Whitfield's sermon in a letter)

Hurrah! Hurrah! Hurrah! For our people who stood up like men and women in the face of trouble, stood the abuse of law enforcers who guard the camps at night. You have put your condition before the world.

I know how they tried to starve you to death.

I know how they drove you from the highway to hide you from the world.

I know how they cursed you.

I know they told you that I had forsaken you.

I know they tried to make you lose faith in me and the union.

I didn't leave you in trouble because I was afraid. I would willingly die with you, but I left because they were getting ready to lynch me because I put our condition in the spotlight and let the world get a picture of the system under which we have worked all these years.

I could not help you dead or in jail. They wanted to murder me because I succeeded in doing something no other Negro leader has ever done. And I proved that our people stick together if they have a leader that they can trust, a leader that won't sell them out.

Everybody from St. Louis to New York is going to Washington to fight it out with the administrators, and we may talk it over with the President himself.

They scattered you all over the country and packed you in towns, in barns, and churches and on levees, but we know where you are and we will get you just as soon as we get what we are after. And that is LAND for the LANDLESS, HOMES FOR THE HOMELESS, AND FREEDOM FOR THE WAGE SLAVES.

AND ALWAYS REMEMBER THIS: YOU HAVE WON. IT WILL TAKE A LITTLE TIME TO GET WHAT YOU FOUGHT FOR, BUT YOU WILL SOON SEE THAT YOU HAVE WON. SO STICK TO THE SOUTHERN TENANT FARMERS' UNION.

From one that has lost all that he had for his people both white and black.

(O. H. Whitfield, Vice President, Southern Tenant Farmers' Union, February 5, 1939, Memphis, Tennessee)

Storyteller Four:

The people in the concentration camps suffered through the winter of 1939. Near starvation in mid-June, four hundred destitute sharecroppers, the remnant of the protesters, were moved by union trucks to ninety-three acres of land purchased for them by the union; the Committee for the Rehabilitation of the Sharecroppers; students from Lincoln University, Jefferson City, Missouri; and contributions from people around the country who cared about them. The new integrated farm community was called Cropperville Camp. It was near Harviell, Missouri, southwest of Poplar Bluff. Cropperville existed until 1945. Today, the land and the cemetery are owned by an alliance of African American Baptist churches and used for a children's summer camp.

Students at new schoolhouse in Cropperville (1939)

Photo by Arthur Witman. Used by permission and courtesy of the State Historical Society of Missouri.

ACTIVISM
Out of Despair . . . Individuals, Students, and the Community Create "Cropperville"
(Part 3 of DVD, 36:42–56:00 min)

Introduction

After the protest on Highways 60 and 61, protesters with nowhere else to go were moved to the spillway and other out-of-the-way places near Poplar Bluff, Missouri. Owen Whitfield was able to acquire ninety-three acres of hilly woodland and unusable land. He and his followers set up their own community called "Cropperville."

Outcomes

As a result of this lesson, students will be able to:

1. Analyze the photos of Cropperville and place them in context.

2. Identify specific jobs and activities at Cropperville after analyzing the photos.

3. Use their literacy skills to talk and write about day-to-day life in Cropperville.

Standards

This lesson plan meets the standards in literacy and social studies in the areas of Key Ideas and Details; Craft and Structure; Integration of Knowledge and Ideas; and Range of Reading and Level of Text Complexity.

Standards of Learning Based on History's Habits of Mind (NCHE)

1. Recognize the importance of individuals who have made a difference in history and the significance of personal character for both good and ill.

2. Appreciate the force of the nonrational, the irrational, and the accidental in history and human affairs.

3. Understand the relationship between geography and history as a matrix of time and place, as a context for events.

Materials

- Eight photos of Cropperville

- "Cropperville" reader's theater script

- Cropperville Memories and Oral Histories

- Word bank created by the class, small groups, or an individual student for descriptive narrative

Strategy

1. Students will have viewed *Oh Freedom After While* (Part 3 of DVD, 36:42–56:00 min).

2. Review the events of how Cropperville was formed from the documentary.

3. Ask students to work individually or in groups with the eight Witman photographs.

4. Analyze the photos of Cropperville and place them in sequential order or context. Use the primary source photo analysis worksheet from the National Archives to assist with analysis.

5. Ask the students to identify specific jobs and activities at Cropperville after analyzing the photos.

6. Use historical thinking skills to pique their interest and to dig deep into the story of "everyday life" in Cropperville.

7. Allow students individually or in groups to use their literacy skills to write about the day-to-day life in Cropperville with a one-page narrative.

8. Share the narratives in class verbally or in a class journal, or post photos and narratives on the class website.

9. Call the class to action through participation in the reader's theater production of "Cropperville," about the protesters' new settlement on ninety-three acres.

10. Student volunteers will practice a quick read of roles with the teacher-director. (The rest of the class will have the reader's theater script in front of them to read along.)

11. The teacher will guide the entire class with the reader's theater script.

12. Compare and contrast their reader's theater script experience with the narratives the students previously constructed.

13. Ask the students to read, review, and reflect on "Ten Million Sharecroppers," by Mildred G. Freed, *The Crisis*, December 1939.

Primary Sources

Cropperville Photo Key:

Cropperville photo 1: Camp meeting

Cropperville photo 2: Cropperville residents picking beans in field

Cropperville photo 3: Quaker student meeting with Cropperville residents

Cropperville photo 4: Two girls pumping water at well

Cropperville photo 5: Children holding hands at meeting

Cropperville photo 6: Man plowing fields

Cropperville photo 7: Young girl barefoot on Cropperville road

Cropperville photo 8: Cropperville residents and Quakers building new one room
schoolhouse near well

Camp meeting

Photo by Arthur Witman. Used by permission and courtesy of the State Historical Society of Missouri.

Cropperville residents picking beans in field

Quaker student meeting with Cropperville residents

Photos by Arthur Witman. Used by permission and courtesy of the State Historical Society of Missouri.

Two girls pumping water at well

Children holding hands at meeting

Photos by Arthur Witman. Used by permission and courtesy of the State Historical Society of Missouri.

Man plowing fields

Young girl barefoot on Cropperville Road

Photos by Arthur Witman. Used by permission and courtesy of the State Historical Society of Missouri.

Cropperville residents and Quakers building new one-room schoolhouse near well

Photo by Arthur Witman. Used by permission and courtesy of the State Historical Society of Missouri.

"CROPPERVILLE"
A Community for Homeless Sharecroppers
Reader's Theater by Lynn Rubright

Directions:

1. Select students to participate in this reader's theater on life in Cropperville.

2. Assign the eight roles to students based on oral histories from Owen (Whit) Whitfield (preacher and activist); Fannie Cook (social activist); Thad Snow (planter); Hollis (volunteer Quaker worker); Shirley Whitfield (Owen's daughter); Mikki Whitfield (Owen's daughter); Josie Whitfield (Owen's daughter); Zella Whitfield (Owen's wife).

3. Do a quick run-through before the actual performance in class.

4. Project pictures of Cropperville on the wall as the script is read by students.

June 1939

Owen Whitfield: (on telephone with Fannie Cook)
Miss Cook! We got it. We got our land! After surviving six months mostly out in the cold! We got ninety-three acres to call our own over near Poplar Bluff, Missouri.

Fannie Cook:
But how?

Owen Whitfield:
The union helped us find land we could afford. It's been paid for by the union and the Committee for Rehabilitation of the Sharecroppers up in St. Louis. Students from Lincoln University donated some money. So did lots of other folks who knew what we were up against down here. A dollar here, a dollar there.

Fannie Cook:
That's wonderful, Whit, but how are you going to transport four hundred men, women, and children over one hundred miles west to Poplar Bluff?

Owen Whitfield:
We already done it. The union brought them, black and white together, in a caravan of trucks. We calling the new community Cropperville Camp.

Fannie Cook:
But, Whit, where are they going to live? What are they going to eat? How will they survive?

Owen Whitfield:
We got some tents. The union pledged enough rations of salt pork, grits, and beans to keep us alive until we can make gardens and clear the land and till some fields. And we got axes. We gonna chop down trees and make ourselves shacks from barrel staves somebody donated. And Quakers from the Friends Service Committee are sending young folk to help us build a school.

Looking Back Several Years Later

Hollis:

By the time we came to Cropperville in June 1941 to help build a school, most folks had constructed little shacks for homes. Some still lived in leaky tents. But there were lots of other problems to help solve. Outhouses were poorly constructed and raw sewage was polluting drinking water. These folks were in danger of dying of typhoid. And until they started taking quinine, several of the volunteers suffered from malaria.

Zella Whitfield:

Hollis, honey, we knew things weren't perfect in Cropperville, and we had a ways to go to make them right. But God sent you Quakers to build a schoolhouse and help with health problems. We already had small gardens and fields growing corn, so we weren't starving anymore. And we had pigs, goats, chickens, and a cow. Folks shipped clothes from around the country, so we wouldn't freeze in winter. And our women made quilts. Compared to what they were up against out on the highway and in the concentration camps, these folks thought they were in heaven. Well, almost.

Mikki Whitfield:

We Whitfields had a nice house in Meacham Park near St. Louis. Daddy took us there to be safe when the protest was going on in 1939. I didn't want to leave and go to live in a drafty old shack in a place called Cropperville. Why should we leave our comfortable home and our schools to go down there and clear land and try to farm with those poor sharecroppers? I told Mama I didn't want to go.

Shirley Whitfield:

But we didn't have a choice. When Mama made her mind up to do something to help Daddy, nothin' was gonna change it. So we moved down to Cropperville and learned to pump water from the well, pick beans, milk the cows and goats, gather eggs, and help make butter and molasses. When folks asked if we liked Cropperville, I said I liked the singing, dancing, and playing games. I didn't like the work. No, thank you.

Thad Snow:

I often brought a brace of pheasants or ducks from my hunting when in the neighborhood. Whit sometimes wasn't there as he was union organizing around the country. But Zella was holding down the fort. And it wasn't easy. There were factions, of course. There always are. Grumblers, those wanting control. Both black and white. But nobody, I mean nobody, outranked Zella Whitfield. She had a ministry of her own at Cropperville and everybody knew it. She was a little thing, but she was tough. She saw that everybody followed the rules for behavior that Whit had set down. No drunkenness, no carousing. If you broke the rules, you were out.

Fannie Cook:

When the schoolhouse was done, the local school board donated desks and books. We found an African American teacher. The older Cropperville residents loved learning as much as the children. They came to classes before the regular school began and came again after the kids left. And when they learned to sign their names and could *read*, a politician running for judge donated a piano to the school. He was looking for votes. The way the folks at Cropperville loved to sing and dance, they probably voted for him.

Mikki Whitfield:

We didn't even know we were poor. After chores, we swam in the Little Black Creek. We put on talent shows. We had plenty of visitors for an audience: Fannie Cook, Thad Snow, the Quakers, local ministers, reporters, photographers. My favorite song and dance with my sisters was "Don't bring us posies, when shoesies what we need." That brought a laugh from everyone. Because we really did need shoes.

Josie Whitfield:

My daddy, Owen, even met with President Franklin Delano Roosevelt during those years he was a union organizer. Mama met with Mrs. Roosevelt and told her about how she helped Daddy start Cropperville as a way station to help destitute sharecroppers find a better life. By 1943, most of the young men had joined the army. Others went north as part of the Great Migration to work in factories. Just like Daddy hoped, Cropperville helped folks "move on."

Thad Snow and Owen and Zella Whitfield, circa 1954 *(source unknown)*

CROPPERVILLE MEMORIES AND ORAL HISTORIES

By Shirley Whitfield Farmer and Josie Whitfield McGee
(Children of Rev. Owen H. and Zella Glass Whitfield)

Compiled from memories of the Whitfield children and written down by family members. Edited by Lynn Rubright, 2009.

Introduction:

These stories were sent to me by Josie Whitfield McGee and Shirley Whitfield Farmer. They are based on their childhood experiences between 1939 and 1945 while living at Cropperville, a small community southeast of Poplar Bluff, near Harviell, Missouri. This community was established by their parents, Reverend Owen H. Whitfield and Zella Glass Whitfield, following a roadside demonstration in southeast Missouri in 1939 during which 1,200 black and white sharecroppers protested unfair labor practices that grew out of the Great Depression.

Presently, the ninety-three acres of land that became Cropperville and served as a way station for about four hundred homeless sharecroppers, black and white, beginning in June 1939, are used as a summer camp for children. The cemetery has been lovingly restored by the Whitfield family and local residents who share a concern that the memory of the people of Cropperville who are buried there shall never be forgotten. The Whitfield Foundation helps with funding this endeavor.

Oral Histories:
"Cropperville's Early Days," Shirley Whitfield Farmer
"Milking the Cow," Josie Whitfield McGee
"Making Butter," Josie Whitfield McGee
"Hog Killin' Time," Josie Whitfield McGee
"Making Sorghum Molasses," Shirley Whitfield Farmer

CROPPERVILLE'S EARLY DAYS

Shirley Whitfield Farmer

When we first moved to Cropperville, there weren't any roads. Except for a few houses that had been built with logs and packed with mud in between, everything was woods . . . weeds . . . vines . . . and snakes.

We had two mules, Jim and Alice, who helped make roads leading into and through what we called the Cropperville Camp.

Some men cut down the trees. Other men cleared the land for big fields for cooperative planting of crops. I remember the men made a piece of equipment that was a triangle in shape made of logs. Railroad spikes were driven into the ground when the mules pulled it up to break the ground. Today such a piece of equipment is called a harrow.

The first years at Cropperville were very difficult. People were often angry. Reverend Owen Whitfield's union sent beans and rice to keep people alive until their fields produced food. Kind people sent clothes and money now and again. Soon there were chickens, pigs, cows, and goats, and Cropperville became a real community of people who worked hard and shared what they had.

Owen Whitfield and Zella Whitfield saw to it that there was discipline and folks followed the rules. If children broke the rules, there were whippings . . . not spankings.

Everyone worked, even small children had duties, carrying water, watching smaller ones that were grouped in one place. Older women who were too old or too ailing would prepare food for everyone.

Evening chores for children of each family consisted of filling the lamps used for light with coal-oil and washing the smoky chimneys of the lamps. Younger boys hauled and stacked wood and logs for winter fuel, especially for those who were older and sick.

But it wasn't all work. We created our own fun by singing, dancing, and playing games and fishing and swimming in the Little Black River which ran through our land. We rolled old tires down a small hill. And we even took turns riding an old bicycle without brakes that traveled fast down that hill.

MILKING THE COW
Josie Whitfield McGee

My sister Shirley knew how to milk the cows and goats . . . even though she was only about nine or ten years old. But it was Mr. Hosie (Hosea Johnson) who did most of the milking at Cropperville. He shared the buckets of cow's milk among the families who had the most children.

When Mr. Hosie left a bucket of milk at our house, Shirley, Mamma, and I poured the milk into large glass milk jars. But first we had to put a piece of cheese cloth or bit of a sheet over the mouth of the jar to clear the milk of bits of dirt, bugs, and hairs that may have fallen into the bucket while Mr. Hosie milked the cow.

The milk was never homogenized, but after straining it, the milk was clean enough for us to drink. We saved some of the rich milk for cream, and to make butter.

The milk was then placed in a semi-warm place where it would "clabber" or "lump" for a few days. That meant a yellow substance—the cream—rose to the top of the jars. It was then poured into the butter churn. Although some butter churns are made of wood, our butter churn was ceramic. We bought our butter churn at the store.

MAKING BUTTER
Josie Whitfield McGee

When the milk had "clabbered" or gotten lumpy from the cream rising to the top—after a few days of sitting in our glass jars—it was time to make butter.

We poured the lumpy rich milk into the ceramic butter churn. There was a wooden top that covered the butter churn with a hole in the middle. A long wooden pole, like a broom handle, fit through the hole. Paddles attached to the end of the pole fit inside the bottom of the churn.

The person making butter had the chore of working the wooden churn handle up and down so the paddles down inside the churn would beat the milk into butter.

If the cream did not solidify into butter . . . then you had to pour the cold water—just the right amount—to help the cream turn into butter. When the butter was formed, we scooped it from the top of the churn, placed it in a bowl, and poured clear cold water over it until it got hard.

Hot biscuits here we come! Now where is Zella's molasses?

HOG KILLIN' TIME
Josie Whitfield McGee

When a hog was slaughtered in the fall at Cropperville, our brothers told us, "It died of a headache. It died of a sore throat."

To be hit in the head with a sledgehammer will give a hog a headache.

Using a butcher knife to slit the poor animal's neck will no doubt give it a sore throat.

The most horrible sight at killin' time was to see my brothers and their friends help the men put the hog in the boiling water.

They would take a huge sharp knife, scrap all the hair off the pig. If no one is sick by now, find a ditch or a bathroom. That's why they don't want us girls to watch.

Next they removed the pig's head.
Then they hung the hog upside down,
Split it open and drained the blood.

They removed the guts (chitlings) which were
Filled with hard corn not fully digested by the hog.
Can you imagine the smell and the sound of hard corn being shot from
   hog guts and
Splattering the outside of the house?

During hog killin' time, I spent quite a while in the outdoor toilet throwing
   up or reading my book. But even so, hog killin' time did not impair our
   appetites for ham and bacon.
All the hog meats were preserved, smoked, and salted for winter and
   stored in the smokehouse. There were ribs, hams, pig feet, pig ears, pig
   snouts, pig tails, bacon,
Salt pork, oil, and grease to use for frying.
We ate everything except the oink!
We even rubbed hog grease on our skin in the winter time.

If you sat next to someone who smelled like a hog, a goat, or fried chicken, it's OK.
It's just your pet returning for a visit.

MAKING SORGHUM MOLASSES
Shirley Whitfield Farmer

In late August or September we looked forward to the day we got off school to
help bring up the chopped sorghum canes from the field to where they were
making molasses. To harvest the sorghum canes, the men made a sharp chopping
instrument I called a machete. We children and women used the machete to strip
the leaves from the canes. Behind us came another crew of workers to cut the
sorghum stalks.

The men of Cropperville made a sorghum mill to make molasses. One part had
two stones that ground the juice out of the sorghum stalks. A long pole was attached
to one end of the grinding stones. The other end of the pole was attached to the
harness of a mule who walked slowly in circles as the sorghum stalks were being fed
into the grinding stones. As the mule walked in a circle, the grinding stones crushed
the sorghum stalks. Juice ran into a long tin trough, under which a slow fire burned
to cook the juice into sorghum molasses.

Since nothing was wasted at Cropperville, even the crushed stalks had a use. They were fed to the mules, goats, and pigs.

The fresh crushed sorghum juice now simmered in a tin trough that was built in sections about twelve inches long. Holes were drilled into each section, so the juice could flow from one section to another as it cooked. The long fire built under the tin trough had to be kept just the right temperature. Too hot and the sorghum would burn. Too cold and the juice wouldn't turn into sorghum molasses. Children had to stay away from the fire, so they wouldn't get burned.

I used to wonder how these people knew how to do this. *Then it dawned on me that these people were descendants of slaves. Some were even slaves in their younger days.*

As the syrup slowly cooked, a green scum formed on top of the molasses now oozing through the trough. We had to rake the scum off, so the molasses could move through the holes section by section. Finally, when it was done, the sorghum molasses, it was poured into barrels where it cooled. Lids were put on the barrels of sorghum molasses and they were carted to the warehouse. Cropperville families had sorghum molasses all year long. As many of the Cropperville families were large, this was a godsend.

Some of the ladies would make hot yeast rolls which we slathered with fresh churned butter and fresh sorghum molasses. Yum! Yum! Mama made the best yeast rolls!

Men, women, and children on side of highway in the evening
Photo by Arthur Witman. Used by permission and courtesy of the State Historical Society of Missouri.

HISTORICAL LITERACY CONNECTIONS
Poetry, Creative Drama and Reader's Theater, and Living History

Introduction

Langston Hughes (1902–1967), a versatile writer in all genres, was mostly celebrated for his civil rights protest poetry. Inspired by Carl Sandburg and African American jazz and blues, Hughes wrote simply but eloquently about the abused, downtrodden, and misplaced in American society, particularly during the Great Depression era. He also wrote of hope and the importance of dreams, themes in *Oh Freedom After While* and the story of Cropperville.

History can also be learned through analysis of primary source materials such as photographs. *St. Louis Post-Dispatch* photographer Arthur Witman documented the sharecropper protest of 1939, and his images were primary source materials used in the development of the documentary *Oh Freedom After While*.

Outcomes

As a result of this lesson, students will be able to:

1. Participate in reader's theater and/or create their own reader's theater scripts.

2. Analyze photos of sharecropper protests and/or Cropperville through creative drama.

3. Create and recite poetry.

4. Research a person involved in the sharecropper protests and/or Cropperville and portray him/her through living history.

Standards

This lesson plan meets the standards in literacy and social studies in the areas of Key Ideas and Details; Craft and Structure; Integration of Knowledge and Ideas; and Range of Reading and Level of Text Complexity.

Materials

1. Strategies for writing poetry

2. Strategies for reciting poetry with Birkman's "Playing with Possibilities"

3. Telling America's Forgotten Stories through creative drama and reader's theater

4. Using living history in the classroom and Roth's "Ultimate Character Development List"

5. Roadside protesters and Cropperville photos with references from Lessons 1–3

1. STRATEGIES FOR WRITING POETRY

1. Create a word bank to use for writing poetry by listing words that describe the situation and the people on the roadside during the demonstration.

   Think about who, what, when, where, why, and how?

2. Study each picture and imagine the time of day, the weather, hunger, and what these homeless people suffered together. Imagine their feelings about relationships with one another—both family and strangers.

3. List nouns, verbs, adjectives, and adverbs. Using the dictionary and thesaurus, expand and enrich the list by clustering synonyms and antonyms. Save this list to expand vocabulary to enrich writing and storytelling.

4. From this list, write a non-rhyming poem or short, traditional Japanese poem: haiku or tanka.

Non-rhyming poem—a poem that does not rhyme

Haiku—poetic form having three lines consisting of five, seven, and five syllables each

Tanka—poetic form consisting of five lines. The first three lines have the same structure as a haiku. The last two lines have seven syllables each.

Both haiku and tanka poetic forms often reflect an observation from nature. The lines do not rhyme, and each line will have a different rhythm. The thought will often flow from line to line without punctuation.

5. Other literary forms that might be explored besides poetry from your "Oh Freedom" word bank are a paragraph, an essay, a letter, an online newspaper article, a blog, a Twitter message, a Facebook message or speech.

6. Research Activities: Using sources from the Internet and the library, research the life of Langston Hughes and choose poems that dramatize the plight of the sharecroppers. Poems for some of the photos might include "One Way Ticket," "Mother to Son," "End," "Dream Variations," and "Dreams." Dramatic readings of poems (both Hughes's poems and original poetry written by students) work hand in hand to bring the suffering of the sharecroppers to life. Simple activities combine oral interpretation, music and movement, creative drama, and reader's theater.

2. STRATEGIES FOR RECITING POETRY

When studying a poem to recite solo or in a group as reader's theater, follow these guidelines:

"Playing with Possibilities: Reciting a Poem" by Dr. Marlene Birkman

Stand and read the poem aloud to self.
Pause before and after the title and after each line.
Join other group members with the identical poem.
Ask one member to stand and read it aloud to the group.

What feelings did you get from the poem?

Which words elicited that feeling?
Did the poem recall a vivid moment from your life?
What do you think is the most important word?
What did you notice as you look again at the poem?
What do you think is the tone of the poem?

Discuss individual responses to the poem.

What feelings did you get from the poem?
Which words elicited that feeling?
Did the poem recall a vivid moment from your life?
What do you think is the most important word?
What did you notice as you look again at the poem?
What do you think is the tone of the poem?

Prepare a group performance of the poem. Use your voices, bodies, and room space to convey feeling.

Present the poem to the audience.
Consider in the reading:
Volume (loud and soft)
Pitch (high-low)
Pace (fast-slow)
Emphasis (stress)
Presentation (solo, two voices, alternating voices, multiple voices)

3. CREATIVE DRAMA AND READER'S THEATER

Reader's theater, a form of creative drama, is a simple yet dramatic art form where readers interpret a script to present a scene to an audience. Traditionally, there is no set or special lighting. Movement is minimal and readers are either sitting on stools or chairs or standing in a makeshift stage area. Students rehearse their reader's theater text until the story flows fluently, demonstrating effective oral communication skills.

Reader's theater can be used frequently in a classroom to enhance reading comprehension, fluency, and oral interpretation skills. For presentation, the readers are often dressed in solid colors to provide a dramatic effect. Reader's theater scripts can be written by students of all ages. Scripts can include a narrator and several different characters' voices. Gesture, movement, and music can be added for a polished and developed presentation.

Students creating original reader's theater scripts must be aware of copyright infringement if using literary sources. Student-written and -produced reader's theater scripts can be based on their research using primary sources and oral histories. Some of these materials may need written permission for any performance outside the classroom.

"Telling America's Forgotten Stories"

1. Students will study the Arthur Witman photographs of the roadside demonstration and/or Cropperville.

2. Students, working in small groups, will choose a photograph from the roadside demonstration or Cropperville. They will discuss, Who were these people? What was their relationship to each other? What might they be thinking or saying to one another? What is taking place in the photograph?

3. Each student will select a person to portray in the photograph and express a point of view of the predicament. Students should try to imagine who, what, where, when, why and how the people got there.

4. Students will create *monologues*. Taking turns, each student in the group tells the story of his or her chosen character in the photograph by orally expressing his or her character's inner thoughts. (Note: These monologues bring the character and the image to life through storytelling.)

5. Students will create *dialogues*. Staying in character, each student will talk to another student who is portraying a different person in the same photograph. Each must listen and not interrupt the other before responding.

6. Students will create a *conversation*. Students, in character, will converse with one another, being careful not to interrupt.

7. Students will create *tableaus*, or scenes, based on the above activities (point of view, monologues, dialogues, body language, and conversations) by improvising tableaus from the photographs.

8. Students will share their tableaus with other groups in class. A simple "set" can be created by projecting the group's photograph on the wall, adding gesture, movement, and music.

9. Students will then craft a script based on their scenes to be used as reader's theater.

10. Students may use the existing reader's theater scripts in the curriculum guide:

    • Lesson 1: "Oh Freedom After While," page 25

    • Lesson 2: "In Plain Sight: Sharecropper Protest on Highways 60 and 61," page 41

    • Lesson 2: "Out of Sight: Sharecropper Refugee Camps in 1939, Southeast Missouri," page 43

    • Lesson 3: "'Cropperville': A Community for Homeless Sharecroppers," page 54

4: USING LIVING HISTORY IN THE CLASSROOM

Overview

Living history is "a simulation of life in another time and used for research, interpretation, and play" according to Jay Anderson. Carl Becker describes it as "a history that does work in the world and influences the course of history." Scott Magelssen posits, "A form of theater in which participants use performance to create a world, tell a story, entertain, and teach lessons." Arthur Hazelius's definition seems particularly apt: "A living museum that . . . depicts folklife through its living characteristics." And Stacy Roth's tenets provide a valuable guide to pedagogy. She says, "Living history interpreters . . . must be historians, anthropologists and effective teachers."

Directions

1. The purpose is to provide the student with an opportunity to conduct research on a person from the past using primary sources, documents, and artifacts to bring that person to life using first-person interpretation.

2. Students should select a person from the *Oh Freedom After While* documentary or any other people mentioned in this curriculum guide to conduct research on some aspect of his or her life.

3. Students will conduct their research using primary sources including artifacts, documents, diaries, letters, and other sources. They may also interview authorities on their specific person.

4. Students will do an introduction to set the stage and provide background information for two minutes. They will then present their person in first person to the class for five minutes. They are to portray an event in their life. Finally, they will answer questions their classmates may have for an additional five minutes.

5. Students should dress in clothing that is appropriate to their person, bring in artifacts or reproductions, and provide background information to their audience to set the stage.

6. Students should pay close attention to "The Ultimate Character Development List: Spheres of Presentation" handout (see page 72): personal, local, occupational, stational, or wider. Students should master presentation skills with eye contact, appropriate voice, volume, and pacing. Practice, practice, practice!

THE ULTIMATE CHARACTER DEVELOPMENT LIST: SPHERES OF PRESENTATION

From *Past into Present: Effective Techniques for First-Person Historical Interpretation* by Stacy F. Roth, edited for brevity by T. Green.

1. Personal Sphere

Includes what characters know about themselves, the unique characteristics that set one apart from neighbors, and family traits that define kinship and shape worldview.

- Name and name history
- Birthdate
- Birthplace
- Immediate household and/or family
- Residence(s) and habitation
- Your education
- Literacy
- Personal belongings
- Personal health
- Personal habits
- Travels
- Past residences
- Important personal events
- Social skills
- Dialect and speech patterns

2. Local Sphere

Includes what your character shares with others. If your character has traveled, you may have more than one local sphere.

- Your neighborhood and its features
- Local social skills
- Health and illness
- Dialect and speech customs
- Religions
- Customs
- Holidays
- Local lore and jests
- Amusements and pastimes
- Neighbors
- Weights and measures
- Foodways
- Local agriculture
- Local flora and fauna
- Weather
- Local material culture
- Local laws
- Local travel modes and conditions

3. Occupational Sphere

Includes traditional occupations that are a main source of income, a partial occupation, avid interests, and/or other work that may not be a direct source of income but may absorb a great deal of the character's time.

- Occupation(s)
- Domestic duties and skills
- Unique skills or talents

4. Stational Sphere

Characteristics and habits related to class, including social competencies, cultivated skills, dress and accoutrements, dining habits, etc.

- Customs of dress
- Dining habits
- Property and possessions
- Friends and enemies
- Betters and inferiors
- Economy
- Influence
- Social skills

5. Wider Sphere

Knowledge of these will depend on character, social class, education, location, occupation, etc. The higher up the social ladder, the more likely a character would know about events in the following categories:

- World events, past
- World events, present
- Well-known figures, past
- Well-known figures, present
- Inventions and scientific/philosophical developments
- World geography
- The arts
- Music dance
- Literature
- World economy
- Law and/or medicine

REFERENCES

American Alliance of Museums, *Principles of Best Practice for Education in Museums*. (2008). Rowman & Littlefield Publishers.

American Association of Museums, Committee on Education, *Excellence in Practice: Museum Education Principles and Standards*. (2005). 1–14.

Armstrong, Sam B. "Sharecroppers, Ordered Evicted, to Camp on Road." *St. Louis Post-Dispatch*, January 8, 1939.

Congressional Digest, June–July 1993. Federal Labor Laws: Early Labor Laws, pages 164-165. EBSCO Publishing.

Cook, Fannie (1941). *Boot-heel Doctor: A novel.* New York, NY: Dodd, Mead and Company.

Freed, Mildred G. "Ten Million Sharecroppers." *The Crisis*. December 1939, pages 367–368. Crisis Publishing Co., Inc., publisher of the National Association for the Advancement of Colored People.

Freeman, F. M. (2003). *A Song of Faith and Hope: The Life of Frankie Muse Freeman*. St. Louis, MO: Missouri History Museum Press.

Gellman, E. S., & Roll, J. (2011). *The Gospel of the Working Class: Labor's Southern Prophets in New Deal America*. Champaign, IL: University of Illinois Press.

Green, Ted. (Autumn 2005, 2010, 2015 and Spring 2013, 2016). Research interviews at Colonial Williamsburg, Mount Vernon, Sturbridge Village, and Plimoth Plantation.

Gruenewald, David A. "The Best of Both Worlds: A Critical Pedagogy of Place." *Educational Researcher*, Vol. 32, No. 4. (May 2003), pages 3–12.

Handcox, J. (2004). *Songs, Poems, and Stories of the Southern Tenant Farmers* [CD]. Morgantown, WV: West Virginia University Press. (1937).

Hanson, Susan Atherton. (2013). "Walking the Line: Social Media and Interpretation in the Early 21st Century." *ALHFAM Bulletin*, Spring 2013, Vol. XLIII, No. 1, pages 7–8.

Langston Hughes (1902–1967): The Voice of the Poet. commentary by series editor J. D. McClatchy, 2012. Random House Audio, Inc.

Library of Congress. Oh Freedom After While Collection. Memphis, TN: University of Memphis.

McIlvaney, N. (2009). "From the Stacks: Western Historical Manuscript Collection." St. Louis. *Missouri Historical Review*, 104(1), 53–56.

NCHE Habits of Mind. (2013) University Heights, OH.

Penn State Extension web article: "What Makes the 'Good Community'?" (August 8, 2017).

Read, K. (2013 May 1). "Museums Help Students Taste History and Touch Science." *Star Tribune*. Retrieved from www.startribune.com/printarticle/?id=205432921.

Roll, Jared. (2010). *Spirit of Rebellion: Labor and Religion in the New Cotton South*. Champaign, IL: University of Illinois Press.

Roth, Stacy. (1998). *Past into Present*. UNC Press.

Rubright, Lynn. (1996). *Beyond the Beanstalk: Interdisciplinary Learning through Storytelling*. Heinemann.

Rubright, Lynn. (2005). *Mama's Window*. Lee and Low Books.

Rubright, Lynn, O'Connor, Candace, and Ross, Steven J. (producers). (1999). *Oh Freedom After While* documentary. Webster University and University of Memphis.

Smith, G. A. (2002). "Place-Based Education: Learning to Be Where We Are." *Phi Delta Kappan*, 83(8), 584–594.

Snow, T. (2012). *From Missouri: An American Farmer Looks Back*. Bonnie Stepenoff (Ed.). Columbia.

Snow, T. (1956). *From Missouri*. Houghton Mifflin Co., Boston.

Southern Poverty Law Center. (2011). Teaching the Movement: The State Standards We Deserve. Montgomery, AL: Kate Shuster.

St. Louis Urban League time line. Retrieved from www.ulstl.com/historical-timeline/.

State Historical Society of Missouri. (1939). Barnes Papers. Columbia, MO: C. M. Barnes.

Tilden, F. (1977). *Interpreting Our Heritage* (3rd ed.). Chapel Hill, NC: The University of North Carolina Press.

Winkler, Allan M. (2006). *Franklin D. Roosevelt and the Making of Modern America*. Pearson.

Wyman, Richard M. Jr. (2005). *America's History through Young Voices*. Pearson.

Youngs, J. William T. (2006). *Eleanor Roosevelt: A Personal and Public Life*. Pearson.

Zella Whitfield [Obituary]. (1985 October 31). *Bulletin-Journal*, Cape Girardeau, MO.

ONLINE RESOURCES

Here are some online resources and additional content to support your curriculum:

History of the Sharecropper Protest

California Newsreel, *Oh Freedom After While*: newsreel.org/video/OH-FREEDOM-AFTER-WHILE

Library of Congress, The American Folklife Center. The Civil Rights History Project: Survey of Collections and Repositories. University of Memphis. Special Collections/Mississippi Valley Collection: www.loc.gov/folklife/civilrights/survey/view_repository.php?rep_id=1100

Missouri History Museum Library and Research Center: mohistory.org/lrc/collections/archives

Southern Spaces, "Out Yonder on the Road: Working Class Self-Representation and the 1939 Roadside Demonstration in Southeast Missouri": https://southernspaces.org/2010/out-yonder-road-working-class-self-representation-and-1939-roadside-demonstration-southeast

Webster University Library Archives: Oh Freedom After While archive collection (papers, letters, oral histories, photographs, and curriculum): library.webster.edu/archives/

Storytelling and Creative Drama

International Storytelling Center: www.storytellingcenter.net

Storytelling and Creative Drama: www.lynnrubright.com

Poetry Foundation, Langston Hughes: www.poetryfoundation.org/poets/langston-hughes

Living History

American Association for State and Local History: www.aaslh.org/

Association for Living History, Farm and Agricultural Museums: alhfam.org

Colonial Williamsburg Foundation: www.history.org

Museum Education

National Civil Rights Museum: www.civilrightsmuseum.org

National Council for History Education: www.nche.net

National Park Service: www.nps.gov

Smithsonian National Museum of African American History and Culture: nmaahc.si.edu

For further information, contact the following:

California Newsreel for the documentary on DVD

Center for Regional History, Southeast Missouri State University, Cape Girardeau, Missouri

Mississippi County Historical Society, Charleston, Missouri

Missouri History Museum, St. Louis, Missouri

State Historical Society of Missouri, Columbia, Missouri

University of Memphis Archives, Memphis, Tennessee

Webster University Archives, Webster Groves, Missouri

For more curriculum ideas and classroom activities, contact the following:

Dr. Theodore D. R. Green, Professor, Webster University, contact tgreen@webster.edu

Professor Emeritus Lynn Rubright, visit www.lynnrubright.com

ACKNOWLEDGMENTS

Special thanks to the following:

Shirley Whitfield Farmer, one of Owen Whitfield's children

Dr. Frank Nickell, Assistant Director, Southeast Missouri Research Center, State Historical Society of Missouri

Zelli Fischetti, Assistant Director, St. Louis Research Center, State Historical Society of Missouri

Nancy McIlvaney, Manuscript Specialist and Photograph Archivist, St. Louis Research Center, State Historical Society of Missouri

Candace O'Connor, Co-Producer and Scriptwriter, *Oh Freedom After While*

Casey Altieri, Graduate Research Assistant, Webster University

Dr. Marlene Birkman, Professor, Webster University

Dr. Brenda Fyfe, Dean of the School of Education, Webster University

Dean Laura Rein, Webster University Library and Webster University Press

Senior Associate Dean Eileen Condon, Webster University Library and Webster University Press

University of Memphis, co-producers of *Oh Freedom After While* documentary.

Thanks also to Diane Davenport, Susan Grigsby, Greg Weiss, Chris Jones, and Emily Scharf

The authors wish to thank the following organizations and people for permissions and use of their materials:

St. Louis Post-Dispatch; Penn State University Extension Office; State Historical Society of Missouri; University of North Carolina Press; Crisis Publishing Co., Inc., the publisher of the magazine of the National Association for the Advancement of Colored People, December 1939 issue of *The Crisis*; and the Whitfield family, for use of their oral histories.

ABOUT THE AUTHORS

Theodore D. R. Green, PhD, is a professor in the Teacher Education Department, School of Education, at Webster University. Green teaches social studies, living history, and social science courses as well as a field study methods course in Colonial Williamsburg each summer. Green continues to work for the Colonial Williamsburg Foundation, where he has been writing curriculum and training educators across the nation.

He is on the board of directors of the National Council for History Education (NCHE) and the Missouri Council for the Social Studies (MCSS). He has served as a national consultant on more than thirty-three Teaching American History (TAH) grants as well as training park rangers with the National Park Service. Ted has conducted *Oh Freedom After While* workshops across the nation for more than fifteen years. He has also presented on history, social studies, and living history issues at international, national and state conferences.

Green has received a variety of recognitions over the years: teacher of the year awards, Global Leadership Academy Faculty Fellow, and most recently a 2015–2016 Life Guard Fellow with the Fred W. Smith National Library for the Study of George Washington at Mount Vernon, developing national curriculum.

Lynn Rubright, Professor Emeritus, Webster University, is an award-winning educator, workshop leader, speaker, writer, and professional storyteller. She taught her graduate courses—Storytelling across the Curriculum; Creative Expression; Story, Song and Art; Integrated Language Arts; and Film for Children—for thirty-six years at Webster University.

Project TELL, Teaching English through Living Language, was a three-year federally funded Title IV-C program designed and directed by Lynn for a suburban St. Louis school district. Project TELL explored ways to motivate learning and literacy through storytelling and related expressive arts across the curriculum. Her book *Beyond the Beanstalk: Interdisciplinary Learning through Storytelling* (Heinemann, 1996) is used by teachers internationally. The Emmy-award–winning documentary film she co-produced, *Oh Freedom After While: The Missouri Sharecropper Protest of 1939*, and her children's book based on the life of Rev. Owen Whitfield, *Mama's Window*, (Lee and Low Books, 2005), are widely used in social studies and language arts classrooms.

Lynn is co-founder of the Metro Theater Company, an award-winning St. Louis–based children's theater, and co-founder of the St. Louis Storytelling Festival. Lynn worked for many years as storyteller/educator for the Urban Arts Program at the Center for Creative Arts (COCA).

Lynn is a recipient of a Lifetime Achievement Award and a Circle of Excellence Award from the National Storytelling Network (NSN). She received a Grand Center Visionary Award in 2013 for Creative Teaching of the Arts in Education. She was an Outstanding Alumni Award recipient from Webster University.

Children playing piano at Cropperville

Photo by Arthur Witman. Used by permission and courtesy of the State Historical Society of Missouri.

CPSIA information can be obtained
at www.ICGtesting.com
Printed in the USA
LVHW020251180822
726206LV00009B/477